MUSICIANS INSTITUTE

Music Reading
for Guitar
THE COMPLETE METHOD

by David Oakes

ISBN 0-7935-8188-5

HAL•LEONARD®
CORPORATION

7777 W. BLUEMOUND RD. P.O. BOX 13819 MILWAUKEE, WI 53213

Visit Hal Leonard Online at
www.halleonard.com

Preface

Having devoted the past ten years of my life to teaching guitar players how to read music, I have observed one very important fact: No one ever learned how to sightread on the guitar by just practicing sightreading. In fact, if I had a nickel for every guitarist who ever came up to me and said, "I want to get my reading chops together," I would be a very rich man. I usually respond, "Great, but what music are you working on?" The answer is typically a very confused look followed by a response like, "I don't want to learn music. I just want to sightread anything that I want to or need to."

This conversation points out a common flaw in music education with regards to the guitar: the study of musicianship is lacking in most students of the instrument. Ear training, harmony, and music reading (not to be confused with sightreading) are three subjects that should be a top priority for any serious guitar student. These courses, studied separately, will eventually become one large course on music. You will learn to analyze music as you read it; your ear will "hear the notes" before you play them; you will learn to write down or transcribe what you hear or play; and you will learn to compose music at your instrument or from your mind's ear and then notate the composition.

The ability to sightread is a *fringe benefit* that one achieves only after reading and learning a lot of music, playing in many different ensemble situations, learning the fingerboard, and practicing fundamental reading skills.

That said, this book deals with the subject of learning how to read music on the guitar on many levels. We will start with basic concepts of how to read music and end with advanced sightreading concepts. The treatment of the subject is thorough. This book was not written for someone to read in an easy chair; it should be read only from a music stand. I will set reading levels for you and expect you to master each level before proceeding to the next.

This book assumes that you have been playing the guitar for at least two years but that you have never given very serious thought to learning how to read music until recently.

Good luck, and work hard.

–David Oakes

About This Book

There are two different kinds of melodic reading exercises in this book. First there are many "nonsense melodies." These melodies should be part of your sightreading work. Nonsense melodies will require you to go slow and work on pitch accuracy. The second type of exercises are melodies written by great composers. These melodies should be practiced (played many times) and worked up to a performance tempo beyond that of your current sightreading tempos. I chose classical melodies for several different reasons. First, my reading classes at MI generally consist of people who are rock-oriented players and others who are jazz-oriented. Jazz players don't like to read rock tunes, just as rock players don't like to read jazz melodies. I find that classical melodies are a good compromise. Second, these melodies help develop a great sense of four-bar phrasing. Finally, they allow you to use your ears to help you read. You will easily hear and adjust any mistakes.

At MI, we spend four one-hour class periods on each chapter over a period of two weeks. You should be able to master the material in each chapter in two weeks time if you practice the material for one half hour per day—four to five times per week. At this rate, you will take almost one full year to complete this book. You will also need to review material on a regular basis. Systematic review is essential to mastering the concepts presented in this book.

Contents

Chapter One

Basic Definitions

Music consists of two basic elements: pitch and rhythm. These elements are notated using a *staff.*

The staff consists of five lines and four spaces. These lines and spaces are always counted from the bottom upward. To find the second space of the staff, for example, you would count up from the bottom, or first, space and then go up to the next, or second, space.

The very first symbol written on a staff is the *clef sign.* Guitar music is written in the *treble* or *G clef.* This clef circles the second line of the staff where the note G is located.

treble clef

Pitch is the relative highness or lowness of a sound. Seven letters are used to represent pitch: A, B, C, D, E, F, and G. With the treble clef in place on the staff, the notes on the lines from the bottom up are E, G, B, D, and F. The notes on the spaces are F, A, C, and E. Memorize these two sets of letters so that you can quickly recognize pitches on the staff.

Name the notes on the staves below.

E   A   C   __   __   __   __   __   __   __   __   __   __   __   __

__   __   __   __   __   __   __   __   __   __   __   __   __   __   __

Rhythm is the organization of music as it relates to time. One of the most basic aspects of rhythm is pulse, which is a steady stream of beats. A pulse is typically divided into strong and weak beats that repeat during a piece of music, and this recurring pattern of strong and weak beats is called the *meter.* The most common meter divides the pulse into four beat segments. The next most common meter divides the pulse into three beat segments.

Meter is divided in notation into *measures* or bars. *Bar lines* separate each measure. A *double bar line,* a thin line followed by a thick line, signals the end of a composition and is also called a *final bar line.*

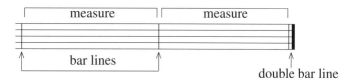

Music notation uses symbols to represent sounds as well as silences as they occur in time. These symbols are called *notes* and *rests,* respectively. The chart below shows some of the most common.

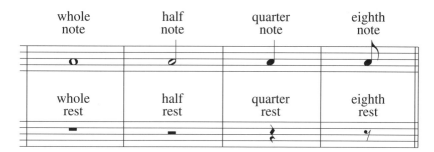

Notice that there are different parts to each note. The *head* of the note can be hollow or filled, depending on the note type. Any note whose duration is smaller than a whole note will have a *stem* attached to the notehead. Any note whose duration is smaller than a quarter note will have a *flag* attached to the stem, and two or more flagged notes may be grouped together by using a *beam.* Stem direction can go up or down depending on where the note is placed on the staff.

The *time signature* is a set of numbers placed at the beginning of a piece of music. The top number indicates the number of beats in a measure, and the bottom number indicates which basic rhythmic value represents one beat.

In 4/4 time, the top number "4" indicates that there are four beats in each measure. The bottom number "4" indicates that the quarter note (♩) receives one beat. This time signature would also make the half note (♩) worth two beats and the whole note (o) worth four beats.

Clap the following rhythm in 4/4.

Three beats in each measure. The quarter note receives one beat.
Clap the following example in 3/4.

Two beats in each measure. The quarter note receives one beat.
Clap the following example in 2/4.

C

4/4 is the most popular time signature in western music, and is therefore sometimes abbreviated "C," which stands for *common time.* When you see a common time signature, count the music exactly the same as 4/4 time.

There are two basic parts to each beat: the *downbeat,* which is the name for the beginning of the beat, and the *upbeat,* which is the name for the exact middle of the beat. When we count eighth notes, the first eighth note occurs on the downbeat, and the second occurs on the upbeat. We use the word "and" to represent the upbeat.

Developing Rhythmic Coordination

Clapping Rhythms

Count the quarter-note pulse out loud in the following examples while tapping the same pulse with your foot. After this coordination feels comfortable, go over these exercises again, and clap the rhythm with your hands. Clapping provides awareness of the *attack* of a note.

More on Eighth-Note Beams

Eighth notes can be written and grouped in many different ways. So far, we have seen the eighth-note flag (♪) and two eighth notes beamed together (♫). Four eighth notes can be beamed together as well (♫♫). This helps the music reader to group beats inside the measure. The group of four eighth notes will still be counted and felt the same as two beamed eighth-note pairs.

Singing Rhythms

Sing these rhythms while tapping the quarter-note pulse with your foot. Singing provides awareness of the *duration* of the notes. Use neutral syllables "dah" to represent long pitches and "dut" to represent short pitches.

Clapping on the Backbeat

Clap on the backbeat (the weak beats on 2 and 4, represented below by the noteheads shaped like an X) while tapping the quarter-note pulse with your foot and singing the rhythms. This is developing three-part rhythmic coordination, which will help you internalize the beat.

Developing Eye Movement

In the early stages of music reading, we tend to stare at the music that we are playing. Later on in this book, the subjects of reading music in two-beat groupings, reading one measure of music at a time, and reading ahead of what we're playing will all be discussed, but first, we must develop the eye's ability to move across the page. To do this, we will start by making the eye jump around and move in different directions in an effort to "force" it to move.

Reading Down and Up the Page

Let your eye follow the arrows in this exercise: Start at the top left corner, and play the rhythms in the first measure. Jump down to the second line, and play the rhythms in the second line, first measure. Continue reading down the page. When you have reached the bottom staff, go to the second measure and work your way back up the exercise. Continue with this pattern until you reach the last measure of the top line.

Reading Backwards and Up the Page

Start with the last measure of this exercise, last beat. Make that "beat 1," and start reading backwards until you have reached the first measure of the top staff.

Start here, and read to
top left corner of the page

Reading in Boxes

Each measure of this eight-bar exercise has been numbered. Instead of reading the measures as you normally would, from left to right, top to bottom, follow the numbers and arrows at the center. Begin with 1, go to 2, then to 3, then to 4—you have just read the outer measures, or the larger box of measures in the example. Now read the inner box—5, 6, 7, and 8.

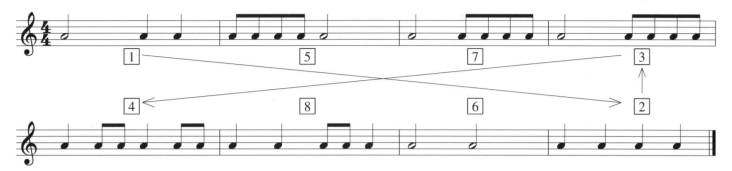

Picking Directions

Most guitarists will use alternate picking for everything that they play or improvise; however, picking directions are different when reading music. We want the downstrokes and upstrokes of the pick to coincide with the downbeats and upbeats of the music. At the rhythmic level of the eighth note, the pick should play a downstroke on every downbeat and an upstroke on every upbeat—so that the pick travels in the same direction and is synchronized with the tapping foot. As we add different types of rhythms, we will learn how the right-hand picking directions will be affected.

Use the note A on the fourth string, seventh fret to play the following exercise.

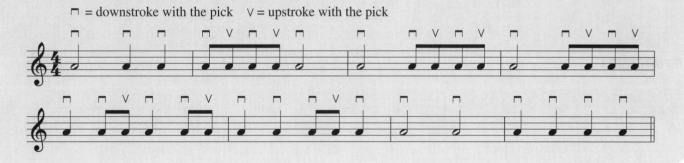

Summary

You may have noticed that we haven't used our guitars very much to read these rhythms. This is because rhythmic coordination needs to be developed away from our instrument and internalized. The coordination techniques we have just learned should be used on *all* the rhythm exercises in this book. But don't practice every coordination every day. Instead, try to vary your practice each day by using different coordinations.

- Clap the rhythm.
- Sing the rhythm.
- Clap on the backbeat.

- Read down and up.
- Read backwards.
- Read in boxes.

- Play the rhythm using down- and upstrokes.

Mixed Rhythm Exercises

Practice the following rhythm studies, making up different combinations of the coordinations. Vary your tempos: slow (♩ = 60 or less), medium (♩ = 60–90), and fast (♩ = 90–120). These tempos will change as you become more familiar with reading music. Practice with a metronome, and work to "lock in" your foot to its click.

EXERCISE 1

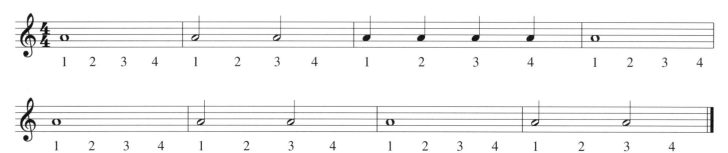

EXERCISE 2

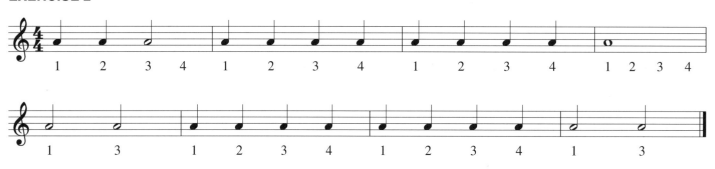

EXERCISE 3

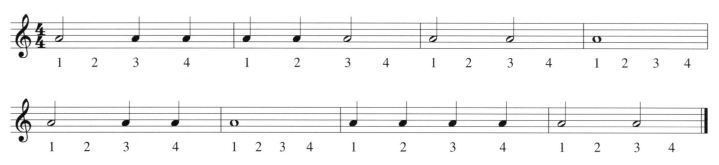

EXERCISE 4

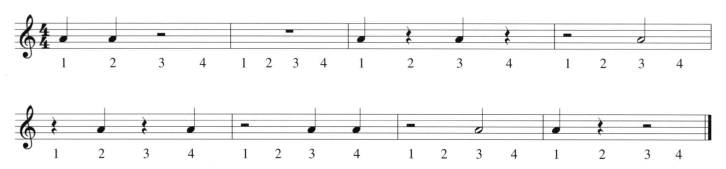

EXERCISE 5

EXERCISE 6

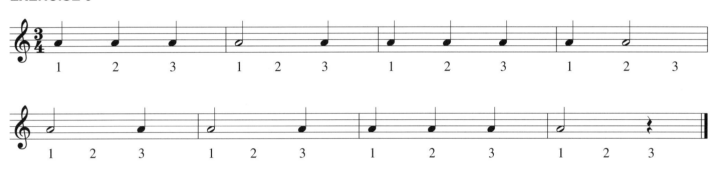

EXERCISE 7

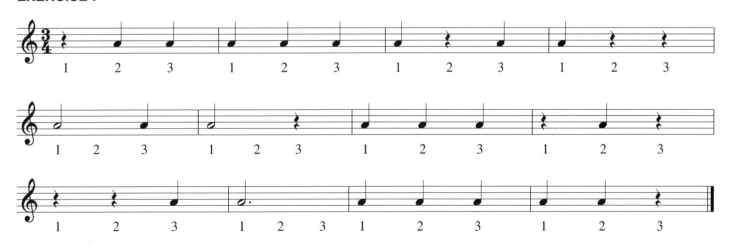

EXERCISE 8

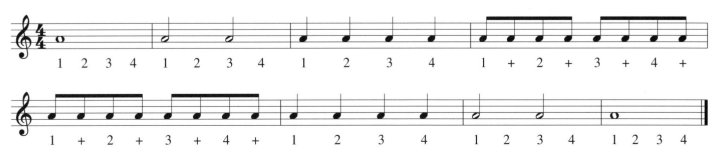

1

EXERCISE 9

EXERCISE 10

EXERCISE 11

EXERCISE 12

EXERCISE 13

EXERCISE 14

EXERCISE 15

EXERCISE 16

Introducing the Fifth Position

We will begin to read music in the middle area of the neck, at the *fifth position.* Most melodies can be played in this range.

The fifth position assigns each of the left hand fingers to a single fret: the index, or first, finger will play all the notes across the fifth fret; the middle, or second, finger will play all notes across the sixth fret; the ring, or third, finger will play all notes across the seventh fret; and the pinkie, or fourth, finger will play all the notes across the eighth fret. These, of course, are very general rules, and we will see many variations in fingering as we progress. For instance, notes found on the fourth and ninth frets are also included in the fifth position, and these pitches will be played either by the hand moving out of position or by a finger stretch involving the first or fourth finger. More on this later.

The Fifth Position

The Second String: E, F, and G

We'll begin our fifth position studies with three notes on the second string: E, F, and G. In the figure below, the Roman numeral "V" shows us that these pitches are all found in the fifth position; the circle number and the line tell us that the pitches are found on the second string; and the numbers above and to the left of the noteheads show us that the E is played with first finger, the F with the second finger, and the G with the fourth finger. The fingerboard diagram further clarifies where these notes are found on the guitar.

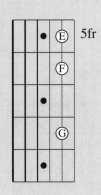

Practice the following melodies by first playing each note while saying the name of the note out loud. Don't worry about rhythm at this stage; just assign a quarter note to each pitch. (This is a basic *visualization* technique that will be expanded upon later.) Then play the melody with the rhythm as written, counting out loud. Don't forget pick directions!

EXERCISE 1

EXERCISE 1 (cont'd)

The Dotted Half Note

A *dot* placed behind a note increases the value of that note by one half. A *dotted half note* (♩ + ♩ = ♩.) is worth three beats. The dotted half note is used often in 3/4 time, where its duration is equal to one full measure.

EXERCISE 2

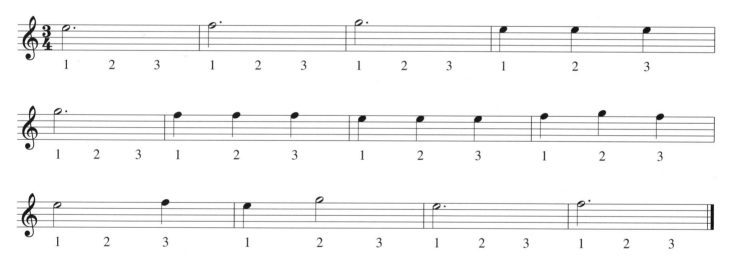

Two New Pitches

The next two pitches that we will look at in the fifth position will be the notes C and D on the third string. Look at the fingering diagram to find C, played at the fifth fret with your first finger, and D, played on the seventh fret with your third finger.

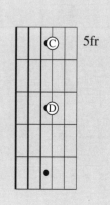

EXERCISE 3: French Traditional Folk Song

Pickup Notes

Sometimes, a composition will begin on a beat other than the downbeat of the first measure. When this happens, pickup notes are used. *Pickup notes* are notes placed in front of the first full measure of music.

There are different techniques for counting in a piece of music that begins with a pickup note or notes. One technique is to count the missing beats of the pickup measure. Another is to count one full measure in front of the pickup measure. In studio or reheasal situations, the leader or conductor might say, "Two bars up front," or if pickup measures are used, "One bar for nothing." If the composition is in 4/4, this first "bar for nothing" may be counted in 2, while the pickup is then counted in 4.

If a pickup note is used at the beginning of a composition, the last measure of the composition will often be an incomplete measure. The total number of beats in the last measure plus the total number of beats in the pickup will then equal one full measure.

Tied Rhythms

A tie is used when a pitch must be sustained across a measure. A *tie* is a curved line connecting two notes of the same pitch for the purpose of combining their time values. The second note is held, but not reattacked. Make sure that you continue to count under a tied note.

EXERCISE 4

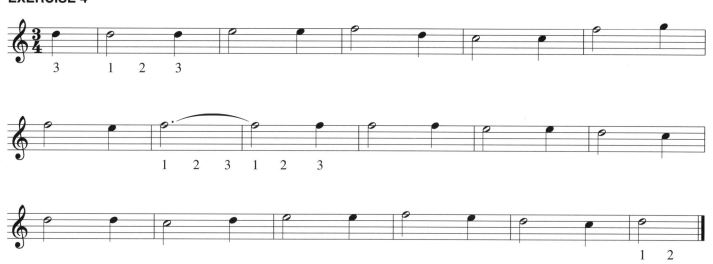

Watch your picking directions. Count out loud, and synchronize your foot with the metronome click while counting. Try reading these examples backwards or in boxes.

EXERCISE 5

EXERCISE 6

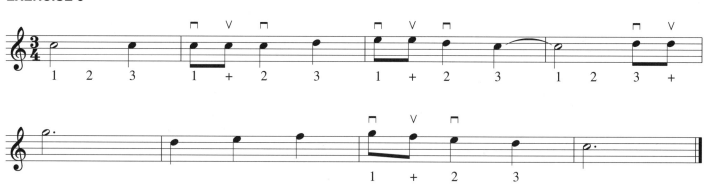

Chapter Two

Upbeat Eighth-Note Attacks

In Chapter 1, we discussed attacking notes on the downbeat; this was accomplished by using quarter notes. We also discussed attacking notes on both the downbeat and the upbeat; this was accomplished by using eighth notes.

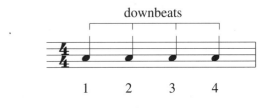

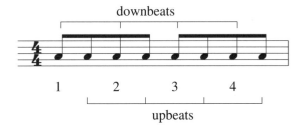

Now we will add the *upbeat eighth-note attack.*

The term *syncopation* means to shift away from the beat, to place emphasis on parts of the measure that are not normally accented. Rhythms that are syncopated are known as *syncopated figures.* If an upbeat eighth note is tied across a measure, it creates a form of syncopation known as *rhythmic anticipation.*

There are several key concepts involved in learning to play this type of rhythm. First, upbeat eighth-note attacks will always be played with an upstroke of your pick. Second, it is important to always feel the downbeat rest by both tapping your foot and counting.

You have already heard eighth-note upbeats in various styles of music; it is important that you learn to associate the sound and feel of this rhythm with what it looks like on paper. The first rhythm below, *à la* the Rolling Stones' "Satisfaction," combines downbeats with upbeat eighth-note attacks, first establishing the beat, then syncopating it.

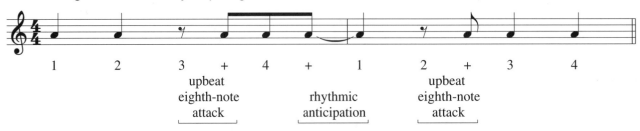

This rhythm, *à la* Cream's "Sunshine of Your Love," follows a similar pattern.

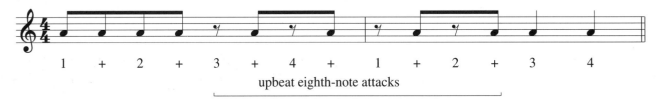

Mixed Rhythm Exercises

Take a few moments to visualize each example before you play it; this is a good habit that will serve you well as the difficulty level of the music you read increases. Instead of visualizing pitches, however, as you did in the last chapter, visualize each note grouping for its *rhythm,* to determine whether you are playing on the downbeat, on the downbeats and upbeats, only on the upbeats, or not at all (rests).

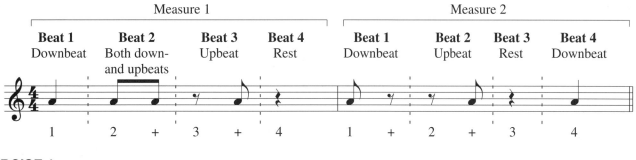

EXERCISE 1

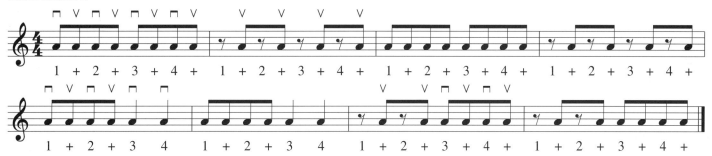

EXERCISE 2

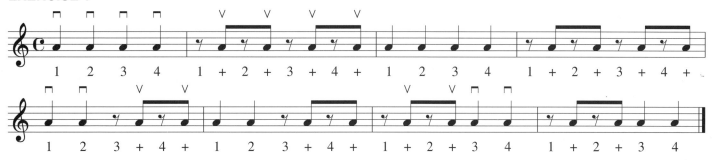

EXERCISE 3

EXERCISE 4

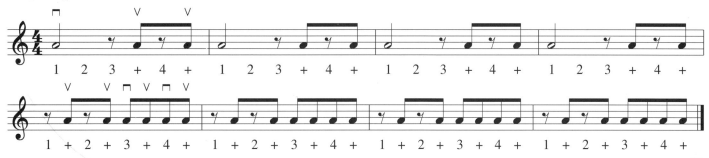

Remember to read down and up the page, backwards, and in boxes. Vary your tempos.

EXERCISE 5

EXERCISE 6

EXERCISE 7

EXERCISE 8

EXERCISE 9

EXERCISE 10

EXERCISE 11

EXERCISE 12

EXERCISE 13

EXERCISE 14

EXERCISE 15

Eighth-Quarter-Eighth Syncopation

The *eighth-quarter-eighth* rhythmic figure is one of the most common syncopated figures in contemporary music. It is very important to be able to hear, feel, and count this rhythm in all tempos.

Notice, in the figure above, that the quarter note played on the "and" of beat 1 is sustained across beat 2. To play this figure correctly, you must feel beat 2 with your foot, and count as you sustain the note. Practice this figure many times. Below is another famous rhythmic motive, *à la* the Beatles' "Strawberry Fields," to help you feel this rhythm.

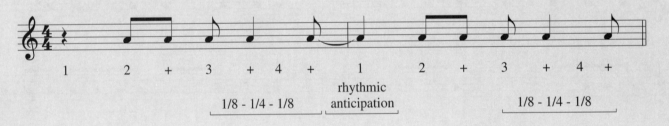

EXERCISE 16

EXERCISE 17

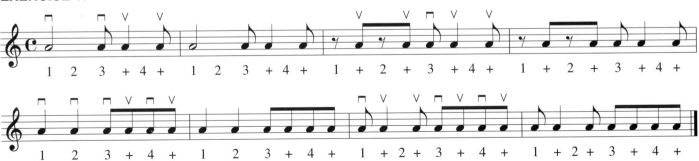

Rhythm Section Chart Reading

Guitar players need to be able to read not just standard musical notation, but contemporary *chart notation* as well. Chart notation is a form of musical shorthand that typically employs chord symbols and slashes instead of specific notes and rhythms, and also makes extensive use of what are called *road map directions*—reading cues and notation shortcuts like double bar lines, repeat signs, codas, etc.—which condense a chart and make it easier to read.

 # Hash Marks

Another term for the slash symbols used in chart notation is *hash mark*. A professional musician will see chord charts using hash marks in a majority of reading situations. In interpreting such notation, the guitarist is usually free to play any voicing of the chord asked for, and any rhythm that feels right within the overall groove. The hash marks below, for instance, tell you to play two measures of Am7 and then two measures of D7. Though the rhythms and chord voicings you choose are open, they must be characteristic of the chart's style and fit in with what the rest of the band is playing.

 # Thin Double Bar Lines

In the previous chapter, we learned that a final bar line—one thin line and one thick line—marks the end of a piece of music. *Two thin bar lines* mark the end of a *section* of music. (You should read through a thin double bar line as if it were an ordinary single bar line.) Musicians find these bar lines helpful when reading a chart because they help the ear hear the phrases. Also, if you get lost in a chart (and believe me, everyone does), finding the next double bar line can help you find the next section and get back in time with the other players. Most phrases are four bars long, and most sections are multiples of these four-bar lengths. It is very common to read a chart where the double bar lines occur at intervals of 8, 12, 16, 24, or 32 bars.

In the figure below, the double bar line at the end of the first staff line tells us that we have reached the end of a four-bar section. We play through this bar line and read the final eight measures.

Repeat Signs

Repeat signs generally occur in pairs. There will be a right-facing repeat sign and a left-facing repeat. These tell you to repeat the music between the two signs before moving on to the next section of the chart. To play the figure below, strum two measures of Am7, then two measures of D7, then repeat. This would be the equivalent of an eight-measure phrase.

A *single-measure repeat* sign looks like a hash mark with a dot on each side. This repeat marking tells you to repeat the previous measure one time. The example below tells you to play one measure of A7 and then repeat that measure one time, for a total of two measures.

A *two-measure repeat* sign looks like two hash marks with a dot on each side. This sign is always centered on a bar line and may or may not have the number (2) written above it. This repeat sign tells you to repeat the previous two measures one time. Remember that most musical phrases are four measures long, so this two-measure repeat sign is widely used. The example below tells you to play two measures of A7 and then repeat both measures once, for a total of four measures.

Every staff of music below tells you to do the exact same thing: play four measures of A7. Each line is written differently, however, using hash marks and different types of repeat signs. Practice this example until you are familiar with each marking and can understand the different combinations of signs that might come up in a reading situation.

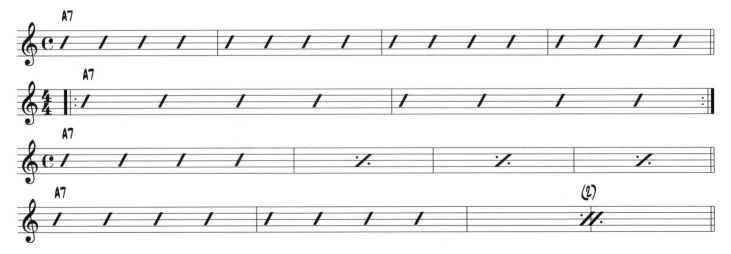

Fine

Fine is an Italian term that means literally "the end." After you have followed all the road map directions in a chart, you actually stop playing when you reach the word *Fine*. *Fine* can be anywhere in a chart. Most often, it will be at the end the chart, under or behind the final bar line. Sometimes, it will be at the end of a section, under or just behind a double bar line.

Da Capo

Da Capo is an Italian term that means literally "the head." Sometimes, a song requires you to replay all or part of the chart again, beginning at the top; the letters "D.C." are written at the point where are you are to jump back to the beginning of the chart. Often, D.C. will be accompanied by another road map indication, such as *D.C. al Fine* (go back to the beginning of the chart and play to the *Fine* sign). In the figure below, you should play through the entire chart, then go back to the beginning and play until the *Fine* indication. (The thin dotted line after beat 1 of the second line, third measure, is an indication to play to beat 1 and then stop.)

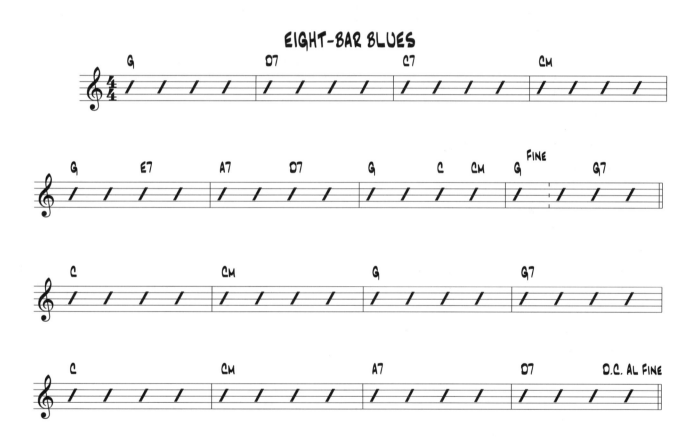

Notice the rhythm of the chord changes in the example above. In 4/4 time, the strong beats occur on 1 and 3, while the weak beats occur on 2 and 4 (the backbeats). In the example above, most of the chords change on the strong beats of the meter.

Dal Segno

Dal Segno is an Italian term that means literally "from the sign." When a chart is repeated from a point other than the beginning—for instance, if a chart has pickup notes or an introduction—the letters D.S. and the sign (𝄋) are used. The letters D.S. are placed at the point when you are to jump back, while the sign (𝄋) indicates where you are to begin repeating from. Often, D.S. will be accompanied by a road map direction, such as *D.S. al Fine* (jump back to the sign, and continue playing until you reach the word *Fine*). In the example below, you would read all the way down to the bottom of the page, return to the sign (𝄋), and continue playing until you reached the *Fine* sign.

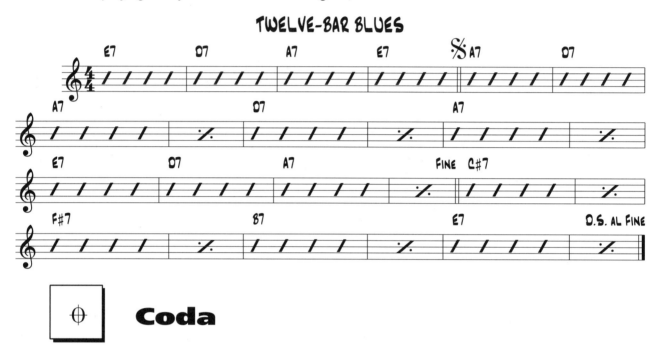

TWELVE-BAR BLUES

Coda

The *coda* is a section of music added to the end of a chart. The first coda sign (⊕) marks the point where you will jump ahead to the next coda sign (the coda added to the end of the chart) and continue playing until you reach the final double bar line or *Fine*. Coda signs are never observed until the second time through a section and are often part of a D.C. or D.S. road map indication. *D.C. al Coda* means to jump back to the beginning and continue playing until you reach the first coda sign, at which point you should jump to the second coda sign at the end of the chart and continue playing until the *Fine* sign or final double bar.

In the example below, read down to the end of the third line, go back to the top and read that line again, including repeats, and then take the coda by jumping to the bottom line and playing until the *Fine* sign.

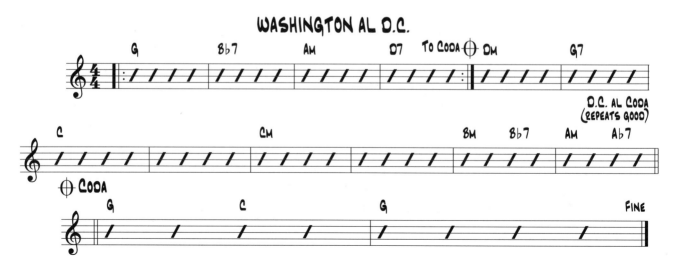

WASHINGTON AL D.C.

D.S. al Coda means to jump back to the sign and continue playing until you have reached the first coda sign, at which point you should jump to the second coda sign at the end of the chart and continue playing until you reach the *Fine* or final bar line. Read the example below.

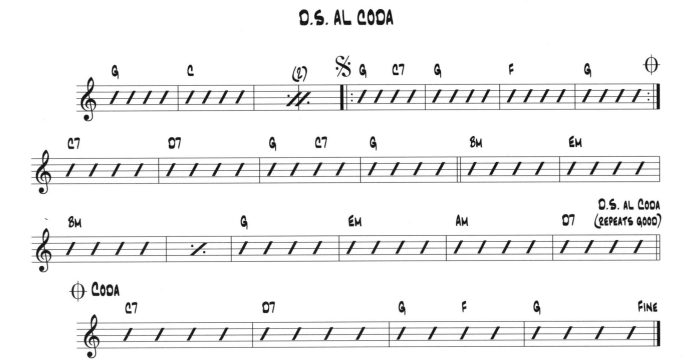

Should you observe repeat signs after a D.S. indication? This is always a tough question, but there is one general rule that you can go by. Remember we said that most phrases are four measures in length, and most sections are eight measures. If taking the repeat means that a section adds up to eight measures, as in the above example, then there is a good chance that the repeats should be observed. Similarly, you could count the number of measures in the section as it was played originally—this section (lines 2 and 3), with repeats, equals twelve measures. Now add the number of measures on the D.S., including the coda. Does it equal the same number of measures?

A Word about Road Maps

When someone talks about "learning the road map of a chart," they are referring to learning the chart's *form*. The first time you look at a chart, you need to be able to answer several questions about it. Where are the repeat signs? Does my eye have to jump back to the beginning or to some other section of the chart? Do I then have to jump forward?

Once you understand the road map, you need to practice following the form until your eyes are accustomed to the movements required to read the chart—this is a direct application of some of the eye movement exercises from Chapter 1.

Notice the use of thin double bar lines in charts. You will find that, most of the time, road map directions will appear at the beginning or end of a section of music marked with a double bar line. Go back through the previous examples and look at their use of double bar lines.

More Notes in Fifth Position

In Chapter 1, we learned that the fifth position assigns each of the left hand fingers to one fret. This works well for most notes most of the time, but there are a few notes that require the hand to stretch out of position to play them. The note B, written on the third line of the staff, is one such note. It can be played either on the third string, fourth fret, with your index finger, or on the fourth string, ninth fret, with your fourth finger. The figure below shows the two places to find B, both of which require a fifth-position stretch.

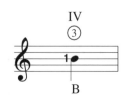

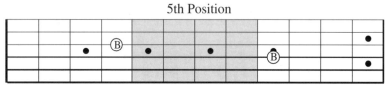

Which fingering should you use? This is an often-asked question, and the answer is both! Your choice of fingering will depend on the direction of the melody and the comfort of the stretch. If the melody is ascending from notes below B to notes above, use the fingering on the third string. The reason is that the notes immediately below B can be played with the third or fourth fingers, making the index finger available to fret the B on the third string.

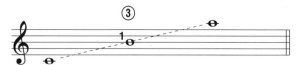

If the melody is descending from a pitch higher than B to notes lower than B, use the fingering on the fourth string. For the same reason—the notes directly above B will be played with the first, second, and third fingers, making the fourth finger available on the fourth string.

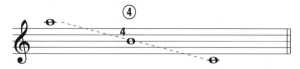

If the melody descends down to B and then moves back up the scale, use your index finger for both B and C.

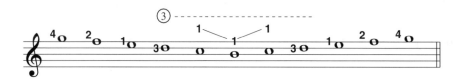

The Fourth String: G and A

Let's add some notes on the fourth string, G and A, into the mix. G will be played on the fifth fret with the first finger. A will be played on the seventh fret with the third finger. Notice that these notes are written with their stems up. Take a moment to add these notes to the fifth position notes that you already know, and then play the figure below.

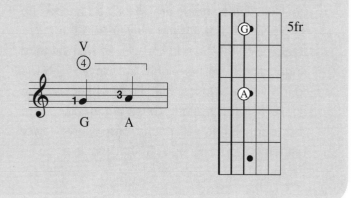

EXERCISE 1

Sometimes, a small shift temporarily out of position will help out a melody. People could make the argument that you are now in fourth position instead of fifth, but it will eventually feel like the positions blend together. You will play different fingerings simply because they are more comfortable. Check out the melody below, and observe the fingerings marked.

EXERCISE 2: "Aura Lee" Melody and Changes

The Fifth String: D, E, and F

Let's add the notes D, E, and F to the fifth position. These notes are all located on the fifth string: D on the fifth fret played with the index finger, E on the seventh fret played with the third finger, and F on the eighth fret played with the fourth finger. Notice that D is written on the space below the staff. These notes, plus G on the fourth string, all sound one octave lower than the D, E, F, and G that we learned in Chapter 1.

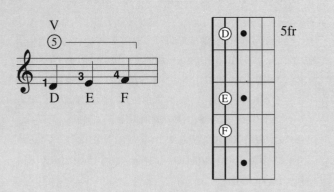

Visualize, then play the following exercises.

EXERCISE 3: Study on the Fourth and Fifth Strings

EXERCISE 4

EXERCISE 5

EXERCISE 6

EXERCISE 7: American Folk Song

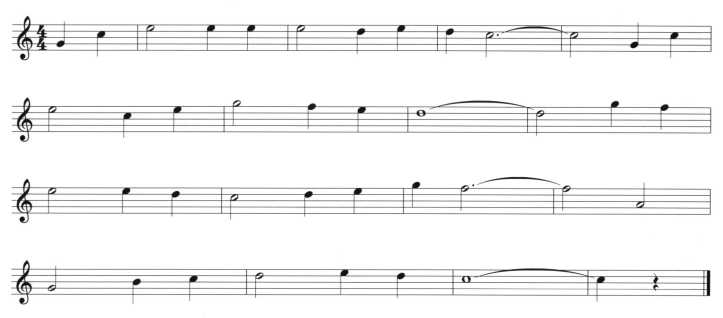

EXERCISE 8: Another American Folk Song

EXERCISE 9

EXERCISE 10

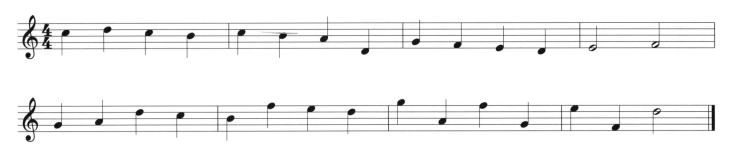

EXERCISE 11

Chapter Three

 ## Sixteenth Notes

A quarter note can be divided into two eighth notes or four sixteenth notes. A *sixteenth* note looks like an eighth note but with an extra flag or beam. To count sixteenth notes, we will need to articulate each part of the beat; just as with eighth notes we used a number to represent the downbeat and "+" to represent the upbeat, when counting sixteenth notes, we use "e" and "a" to represent the other parts of the beat.

Eighth notes and sixteenth notes can also be beamed together. This makes it easier for us to read quarter-note rhythm groups. When we read groups that include sixteenth notes, we will count sixteenth notes throughout the entire beat.

Mixed Rhythm Exercises

Sing, clap, and play the following exercises. Use the coordination exercises listed in Chapter 1. Exercises 1–6 use the new sixteenth-note rhythm combined with Chapter 1 rhythms.

EXERCISE 1

EXERCISE 2

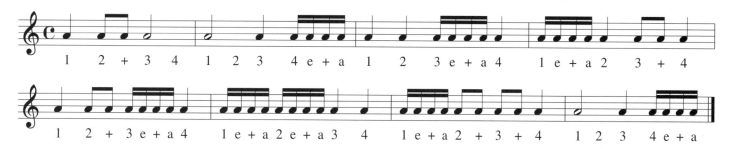

EXERCISE 3

1   2   3   1 + 2   3 e + a 1 e + a 2   3 e + a 1   2   3 +

1   2   3 e + a 1 e + a 2   3 +   1   2   3   1   2 e + a 3

EXERCISE 4

EXERCISE 5

EXERCISE 6

Exercises 7–10 combine sixeenth-note rhythms with the upbeat eighth-note rhythms from Chapter 2. Watch your counting and your picking directions.

EXERCISE 7

EXERCISE 8

EXERCISE 9

EXERCISE 10

Exercises 11–14 combine sixteenth-note rhythms beamed together with eighth notes. Again, watch your counting and your picking directions.

EXERCISE 11

EXERCISE 12

EXERCISE 13

EXERCISE 14

More Chart Organization

In Chapter 2, we discussed the road map of a chord chart. We looked at the different ways material could be repeated and how that affected the way you read the chart. In this chapter, we will continue to look at different elements of chart reading.

 # Endings with Repeats

Often, a section needs to be repeated but will have different phrases at the end of each repetition. When this happens, *multiple endings* are used along with the repeat sign. An ending consists of both a bracket and a number; the number tells you on which pass to use the ending.

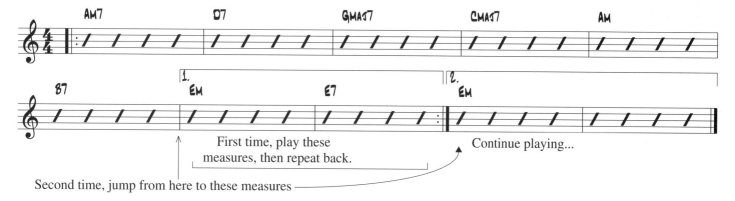

Measure Numbers and Section Letters

Often, the measures of a chart are numbered to help rehearsals flow more smoothly. These *measure numbers* are usually placed at the beginning of each line, above the staff, but they may also appear below the staff, underneath each measure, or above each staff placed in boxes. *Section letters* are also used to simplify rehearsals. They are written above the staff, at the start of each new section, and are enclosed in boxes to distinguish them from chord symbols.

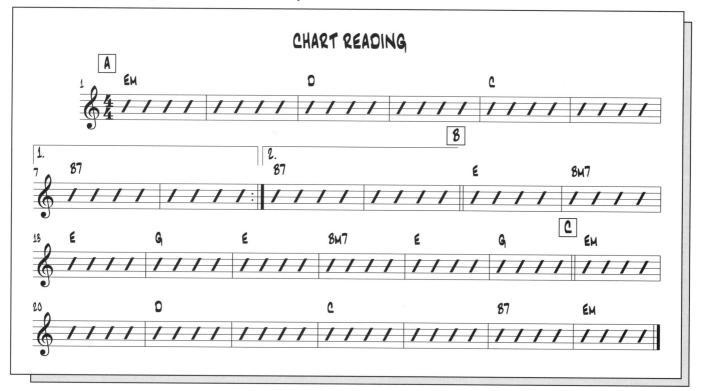

32-Bar Song Form

32-bar song form is one of the most popular forms that songwriters use to compose music. As chart readers, we need a strong understanding of it. Typically, 32-bar song form can be broken down into four eight-bar phrases. The first eight bars are called the *head* of the tune and are marked as section A. This section is repeated in the next eight-bar phrase, often with a different ending. The third phrase is a contrasting section known as the *bridge*. The bridge is usually marked as section B. The final eight-bar phrase is a restatement of the head or A section. Sometimes, this section is marked with the letter C.

The 32-bar song is a truly American form, which can be traced back to such turn-of-the-century composers as Cole Porter, George Gershwin, and Jerome Kern. Countless jazz standards and country tunes—even the most memorable hits of the Beatles—were composed using this form. Musicians today don't ignore these roots; it remains a very common form.

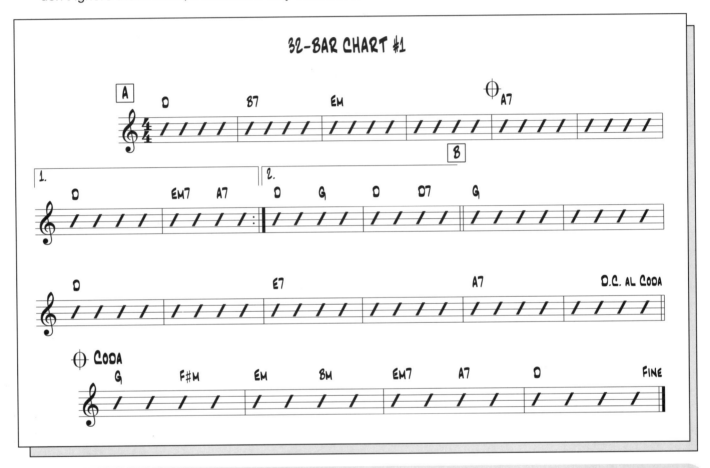

Rhythm Guitar Notation

In contemporary chart notation, when specific rhythms are needed from the guitarist, special noteheads are used by the composer. This special *rhythm guitar notation* is more detailed than slash notation, yet keeps the reader from confusing when to play pitches and when to strum chords. With this method of notation, a quarter note or smaller note value is represented with a short slash attached to a stem, and a half note or larger is represented by a diamond-shaped notehead. Flags and beams are the same as in standard notation.

Introductions

Frequently, a short section (usually four to eight bars) is played at the very beginning of a chart. This section is called the *introduction.* The introduction is usually separated from the song by a thin double bar line and labeled with the abbreviation "Intro" rather than with a section letter. Below is a 32-bar song chart with a four-bar intro.

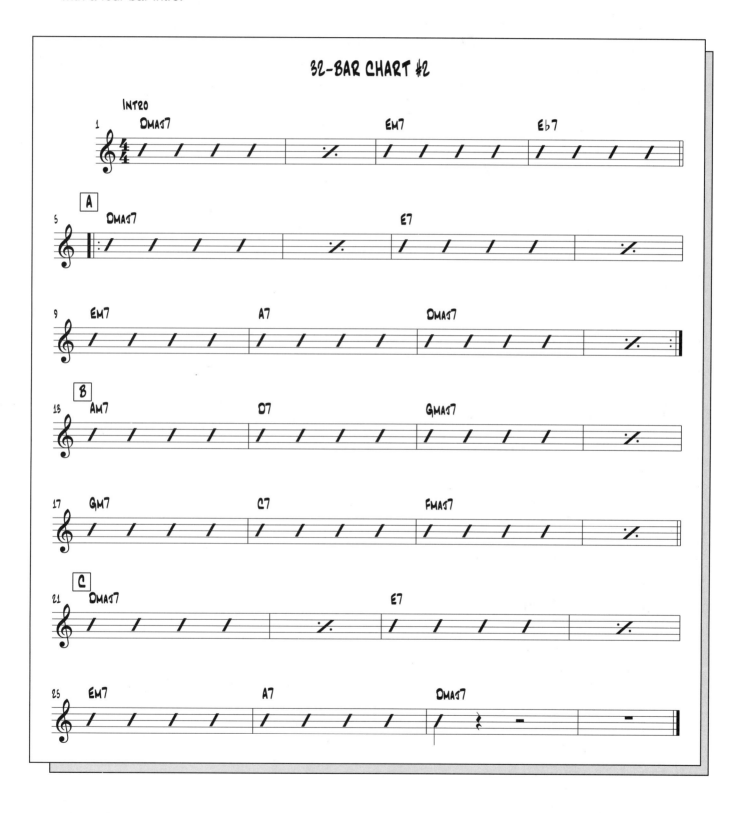

Below is a 32-bar chart with a four-bar intro. Notice that the thirty-two bars are divided into two sixteen-bar sections with repeats.

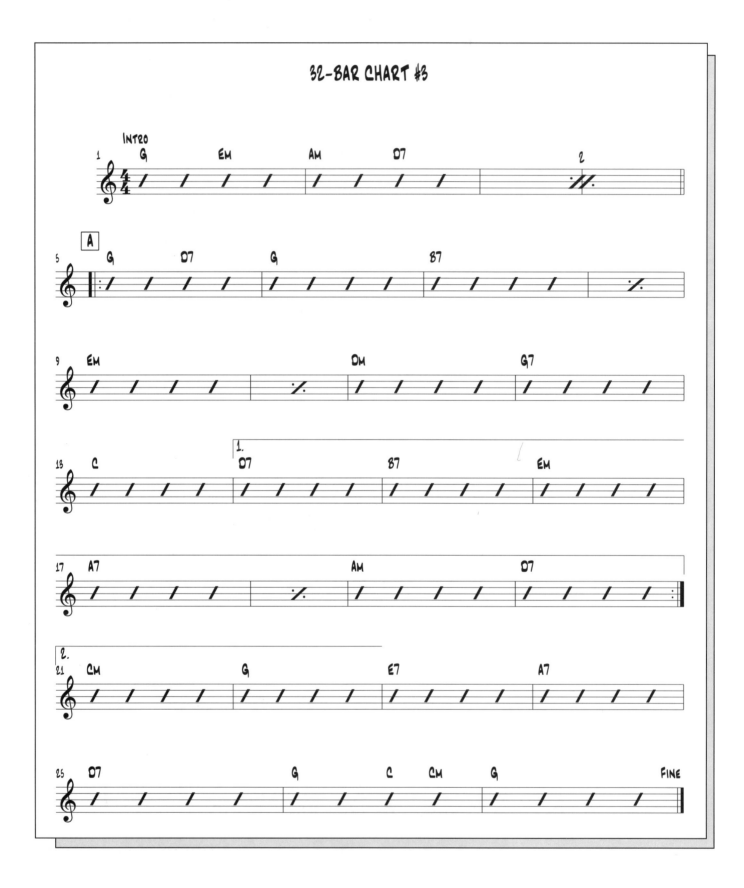

32-BAR CHART #3

Still More Notes in Fifth Position

Music often contains pitches that are higher or lower than the range of the staff. In such cases, *ledger lines* are used to temporarily extend the range of the staff.

The range of the guitar typically extends below the staff by three ledger lines to the low open E string, and above the staff by five ledger lines to the high B at the nineteenth fret (sometimes higher, depending on the particular instrument). The diagram below shows the complete range of the guitar using natural notes, with the range of the fifth position boxed.

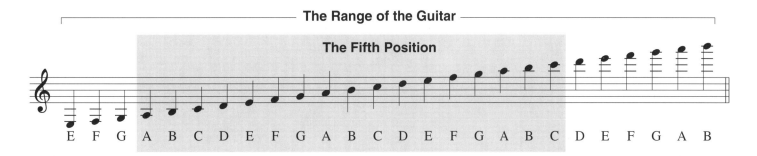

Notice that the fifth position encompasses a large part of the guitar's range. This is why we started reading music in the fifth position. Most standard melodies are in this range and can be read and played from this area of the neck.

The First and Sixth Strings: A, B, and C

The remaining natural pitches in the fifth position are all above or below the staff and use ledger lines. On the sixth string, we will add the notes A, B, and C, written below the staff. On the first string, we will add the notes A, B, and C, written above the staff.

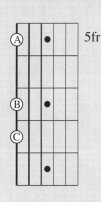

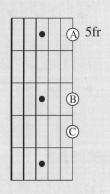

The C Major Scale

All of the melodies that we have played up to this point have been in the key of C major. In fact, if you combine all the natural notes that we have learned in the fifth position, it would form a two-octave pattern of the C major scale. Play this scale several times before playing the following melodies. Play the scale slowly, and name all of the notes as you play. Visualize where the notes are located on the staff as you play the scale.

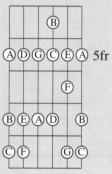

EXERCISE 1

EXERCISE 2

EXERCISE 3

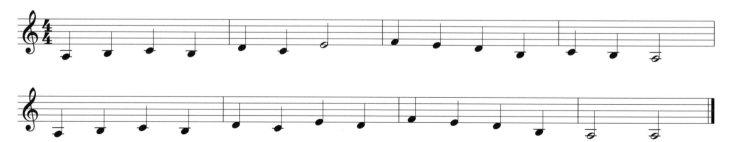

EXERCISE 4

EXERCISE 5

EXERCISE 6

EXERCISE 7

EXERCISE 8

Accidentals and Key Signatures

Accidentals are a group of symbols that modify pitches. Any note can be raised or lowered a half step (one fret) by placing an accidental directly before it.

Sharp (♯)
Raises a note one half step.

Flat (♭)
Lowers a note one half step.

Natural (♮)
Cancels a previously used sharp or flat.

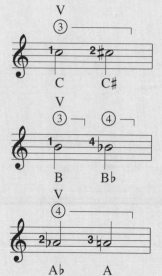

Accidentals apply only to the octave in which they are written and remain in effect only until next bar line; nevertheless, it is common to see *courtesy accidentals* used before notes in different octaves within a measure, or before the same note in the measure immediately following, as a reminder that a previous accidental does not apply.

If an accidental is tied across a bar line, it remains in effect until the tied note has finished sounding. If a different accidental is used on the same pitch, the new accidental cancels the old one.

If a *key signature* is placed at the beginning of a composition (between the treble clef and the time signature), *all octaves* of the pitches included in the signature are affected.

There are many things to check out before starting in on the following sixteenth-note etude. First, look at the metronome marking, $\quarternote = 72$. This is a performance tempo and not a sightreading tempo; you'll need to your work your way up to it. Second, notice that we have one sharp in the key signature and that there are two accidentals that appear in the course of the music—C♯ and D♯. Notice also that the highest pitch played is B above the staff, and the lowest pitch is B below the staff. The notes of this melody fit nicely in the fifth position; however, we will need to make several fingering adjustments. Most of the accidentals and the key signature require a first-finger stretch to the fourth fret, so don't be afraid to shift the hand down to gain access to these notes.

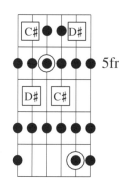

Run a G major scale in the fifth position to become comfortable with the key signature. Then look at where the accidentals lie in relation to the scale. Look for these notes in the music and adjust your fingerings.

This minuet is in the key of G major, and also includes several C♯ accidentals in the B section. Go through the chart, finding these notes and visualizing them on the fretboard. Perform this minuet as a duet with the rhythm guitar part that follows, or just play the two parts separately.

By the way, when a right-facing repeat does not have a left-facing repeat sign, don't panic! This simply means that you should return to the beginning of the music to repeat. Also, notice that this chart only displays the treble clef and key signature on the first staff. This is common in contemporary notation.

Strum the rhythms indicated in the rhythm guitar notation. Notice in measure 4 that there is a chord change with a rest notated on beat 1. The chord change happens on beat 1, but you will still strum only on beats 2 and 3 as indicated.

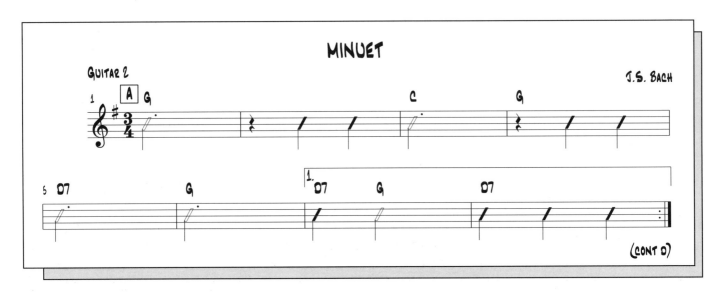

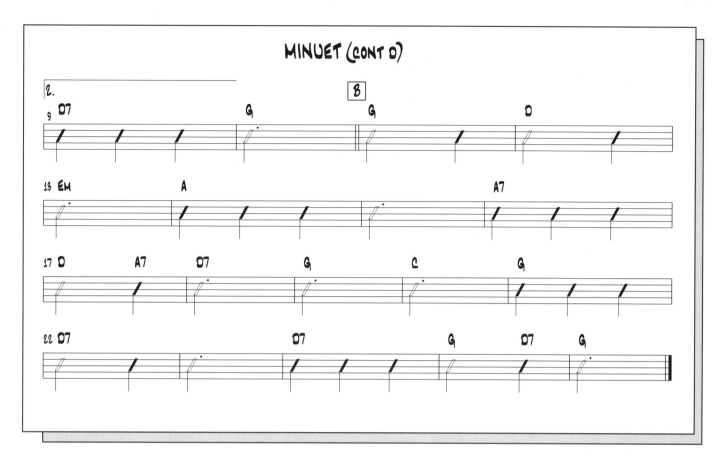

Now try this theme in C major.

THEME

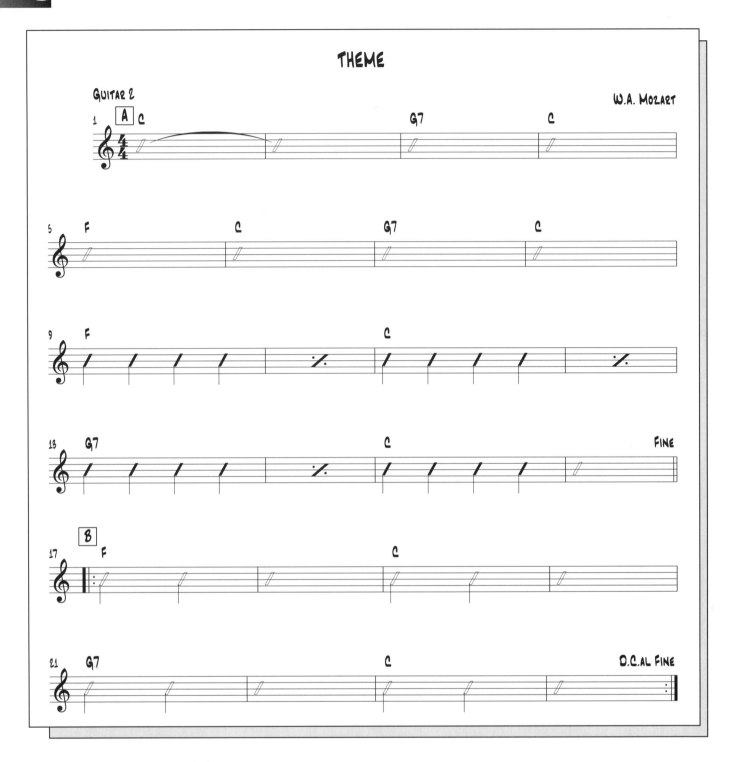

Chapter Four

Triple Meters

As already discussed, 4/4, or common time, is the most popular time signature in contemporary music. The next most common meter is based on dividing the pulse into groups of three beats. This is called *triple meter.* The 3/4 examples that we saw in previous chapters were all in triple meter.

3/8 Time

3/8 is another example of triple meter. In this meter, there are three beats in each measure, and the eighth note receives one beat.

The Dotted Quarter Note

Placing a dot behind a note increases the value of that note by one half. We've already seen that a dotted half note (♩.) is worth three beats. A *dotted quarter note* (♩ + ♪ = ♩.) is worth three eighth notes or 1 1/2 beats.

In 3/8 time, the dotted quarter actually equals one full measure of music. This meter can be counted two different ways depending on the tempo of the music. If the tempo is slow, the eighth note receives the beat. If the tempo is fast, the dotted quarter note receives the beat—you still count the measure in three, but the foot taps in one.

6/8 Time

Although this is not officially a triple meter, its basic pulse has a triple feel. Each measure of 6/8 time looks and feels almost like two bars of 3/8.

Usually, 6/8 time is felt in two, with strong accents on beats 1 and 4. A triple meter that is felt in two is called a *compound duple meter.* Clap the following figure in two while counting out loud in six.

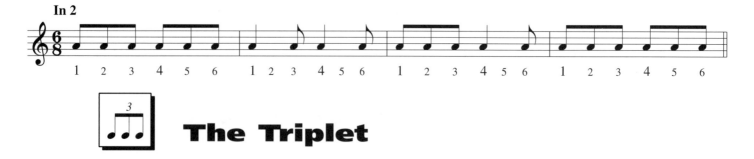

The Triplet

We've already seen that a quarter note can be divided into two equal parts to create eighth notes, and that we can further divide this unit into four equal parts to create sixteenth notes. We can also divide the quarter note into *three* equal parts. The resulting figure is called a *triplet.*

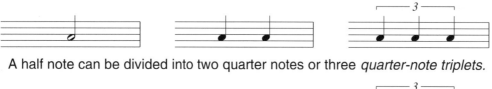

A half note can be divided into two quarter notes or three *quarter-note triplets.*

A quarter note can be divided into two eighth notes or three *eighth-note triplets.*

An eighth note can be divided into two sixteenth notes or three *sixteenth-note triplets.*

These four examples show the same tune written in 3/8, 6/8, 3/4, and 2/4 with triplets. Which is easiest to read? Do any of the melodies sound different?

Picking the Triplet

Picking triplet figures can be very confusing at first, but a few simple rules will help:

- In 3/8 or 6/8 time, the dotted quarter usually gets the beat. This means that the strong beat will be on beat 1 in 3/8 and on beats 1 and 4 in 6/8. These beats should be played with a downstroke of the pick.
- The weak beats can be played with either a downstroke or an upstroke of the pick.
- Any sixteenth-note rhythm should be played with alternating pick directions.

The only exception to these rules would be consecutive groups of three eighth notes. In this case, you should use straight alternate picking. This would place some upstrokes on strong beats.

Mixed Rhythm Exercises

EXERCISE 1

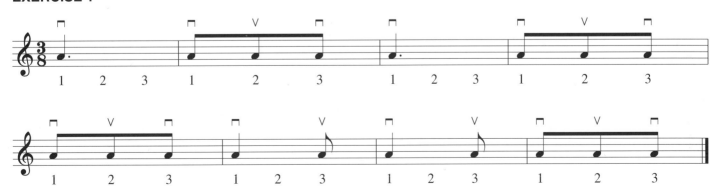

EXERCISE 2

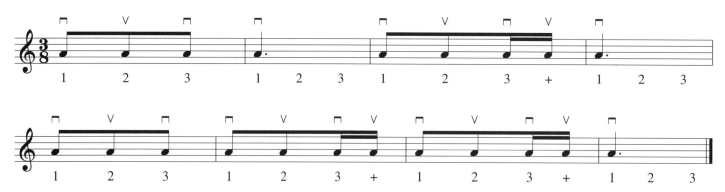

EXERCISE 3

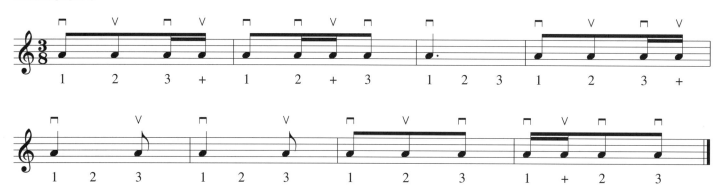

EXERCISE 4

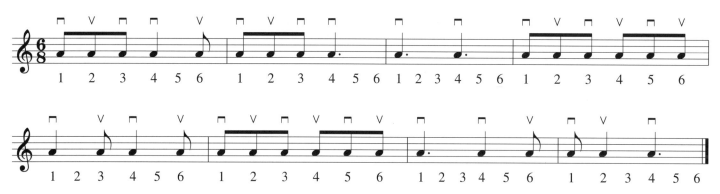

EXERCISE 5

EXERCISE 6

EXERCISE 7

EXERCISE 8

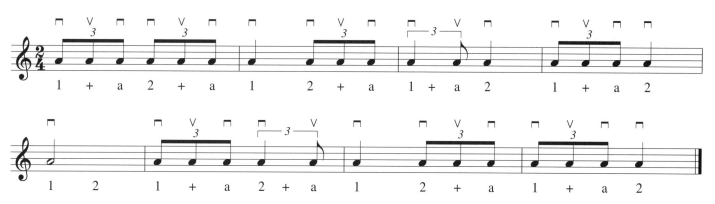

EXERCISE 9

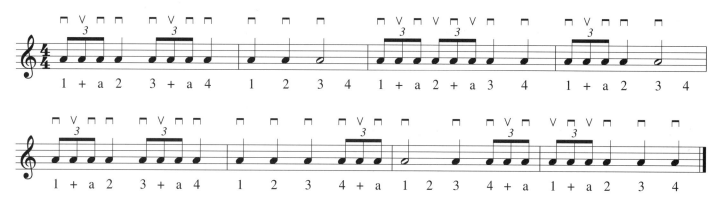

EXERCISE 10

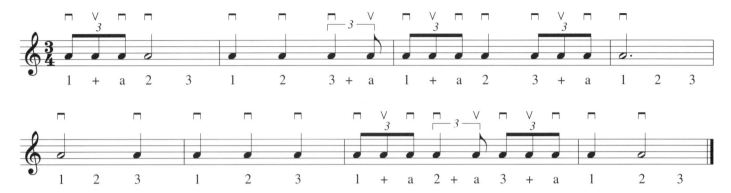

EXERCISE 11

Dynamics and Other Indications

One of the great things about music is that it can express so many different kinds of emotions. Music can be loud or soft, fast or slow. It can gradually become louder, softer, faster, or slower. Notes can also be played differently. Sometimes, they are attacked very hard. Sometimes, they are played soft and connected. Music notation therefore contains many different directions to express these various nuances.

Most musical directions are written in Italian and appear below the staff. There are many to learn, so we will just focus on a few at a time. There are essentially just two main *dynamic markings:* loud and soft. Everything else is a variation on these. Dynamic markings generally appear in a very bold and italic typeface.

> *p*   means ***piano*** or soft.
>
> *f*   means ***forte*** or loud.
>
> *mp* is a variation of piano. It means ***mezzo piano*** or moderately soft.
>
> *mf* is a variation of forte. It means ***mezzo forte*** or moderately loud.
>
> *pp* is a variation of piano. It means ***pianissimo*** or very soft.
>
> *ff* is a variation of forte. It means ***fortissimo*** or very loud.
>
> ***cresc.*** or ⟨ means ***crescendo,*** or gradually louder.
>
> ***decresc.*** or ⟩ means ***decrescendo,*** or gradually softer.

Look at the two examples below. They are each written differently, but both mean the same thing.

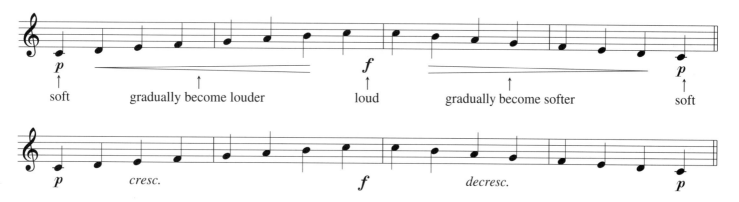

Other directions can appear below the staff. These generally deal with the interpretation of the chart. Often, these directions are underlined or enclosed in boxes. *Simile* is one often used direction written below the staff. Usually one or two bars of a pattern are written out, and then the rest of the section has hash marks in the measures. The word "simile" tells us to continue with the pattern until a new pattern is indicated.

Rhythm guitar directions concerning tempo, groove, and feel of a song can be written in at the beginning of the chart and usually show up on the first staff, above the time signature. Sometimes, they are enclosed in a box. One such direction is the *shuffle* ($\sqcap = \sqcap$) indication. Shuffle is a groove that we have all heard and played many times. It is based on the triplet figure. Notice the two lines below. The first is written using triplet notation; the second is written using straight eighths but with the word "shuffle" written above the staff. Each is played exactly the same.

If "shuffle" is written above a chart with hash marks, you should interpret the hash marks with a shuffle groove.

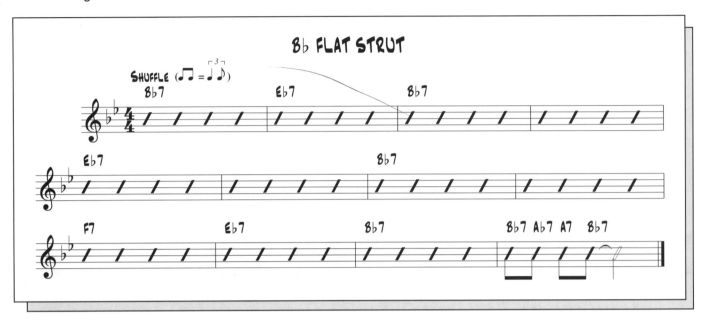

The Multi-Measure Rest

Sometimes, a musician does not play for several measures or for an entire section of a chart. The band might break down to a small number of players, for instance, and then gradually add players back into the ensemble mix. To notate these long measures of rest, the music copyist often uses a shortcut: a *multi-measure rest.* This compressed rest looks like a giant whole rest with a number above it. The number tells you how many bars to lay out.

Fifth Position Review

We will not add any new notes in this chapter, but instead work the notes, accidentals, and key signatures that we have already learned. Remember to go back and read the easier music in Chapters 1, 2, and 3 again, this time at faster tempos.

EXERCISE 1

Beethoven

EXERCISE 2

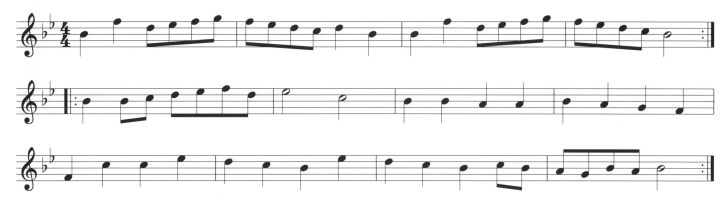

EXERCISE 3: Three-Part Round

* The other parts enter at this sign.

EXERCISE 4

J.S. Bach

EXERCISE 5: Folk Song

Try reading this duet below by switching parts on the repeats. Switch parts on the first ending of both the A and B sections. Keep the part through the second ending and on the D.C.

The following chart is a 32-bar song form with a four-measure intro. The multi-measure rests are broken up into sections. Lay out for the intro and the A section. Come in for the bridge. Check out the measure numbers in the chart below.

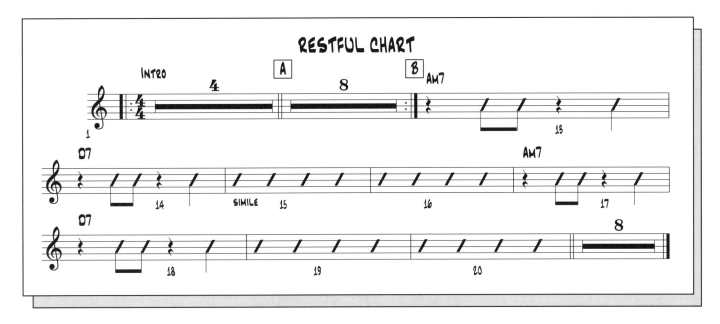

Check out the measure numbers and the dynamics attached to the repeats of the A section in this chart.

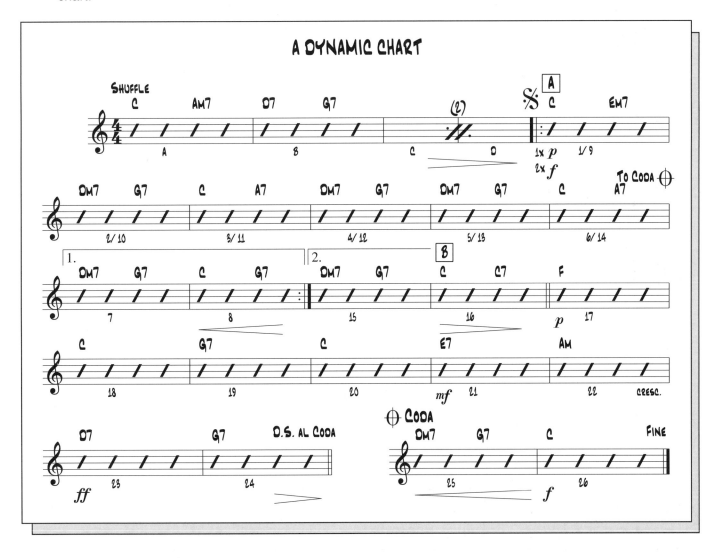

Chapter Five

 ## More Syncopated Rhythms

In previous chapters, we looked at both the dotted half note in 3/4 and the dotted quarter note as it related to 3/8 and 6/8 time. In these time signatures, the dotted note received the beat.

In 4/4 time, the *dotted quarter* is worth 1 1/2 beats. This makes it a syncopated figure, placing emphasis on parts of the measure that are not normally accented. When counting and playing a dotted quarter rhythm, it is important to feel and count all the strong beats in the measure.

Dotted eighth rhythms are usually combined with a sixteenth note. This is a similarly syncopated figure. When playing a dotted eighth rhythm, it is very important that all four sixteenth note attacks be counted.

The last syncopated figure that we will discuss is the *sixteenth-eighth-sixteenth.* This rhythm is the most difficult of the sixteenth-note rhythms to count and feel, but is a favorite of funk rhythm players and important for all guitarists to be able to count and feel. The counting and picking ideas are essentially the same as the dotted rhythms above. Feel the strong beats while counting all of the sixteenth-note subdivisions.

Mixed Rhythm Exercises

These exercises combine rhythms that we have previously worked on with the new rhythms just covered. Go through these exercises and make sure that you see the strong beats in each measure. Group the beats with your eye; this will help you to count and pick these rhythms effectively.

EXERCISE 1

EXERCISE 2

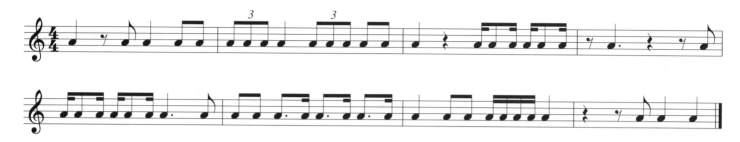

EXERCISE 3

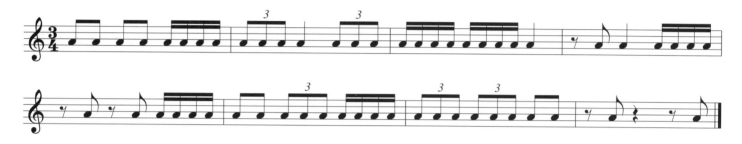

EXERCISE 4

EXERCISE 5

EXERCISE 6

EXERCISE 7

EXERCISE 8

Syncopated sixteenth-note rhythms have been around in popular music for about 100 years. They were one of the defining elements of ragtime music, which grew out of the marches of John Philip Sousa and was perfected in the music of composer Scott Joplin. Joplin died in 1919 and ragtime also died, giving way to the new Dixieland sounds from New Orleans, but ragtime influenced many composers of Dixieland and early swing music.

SUNFLOWER SLOW DRAG
A Ragtime Two - Step

Scott Joplin and Scott Hayden

Choro music from Brazil contains similar sixteenth-note syncopations. Read this melody in the fifth position.

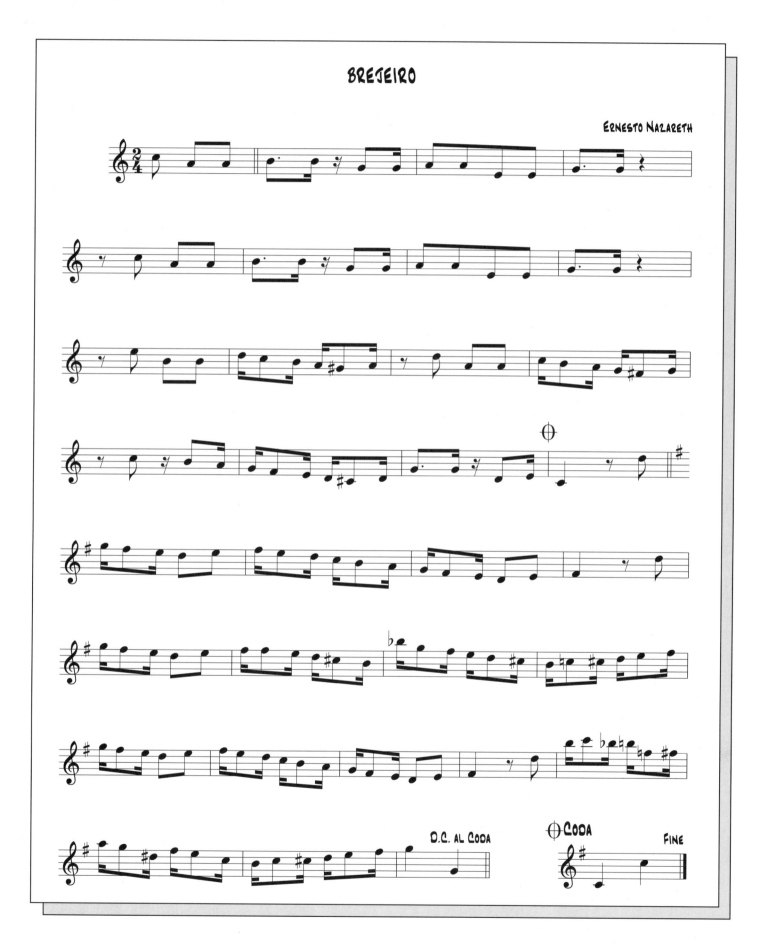

Introducing the Open Position

The first four chapters of this book dealt with reading music exclusively in the fifth position. We will now begin to slowly expand our reading facility by exploring other positions.

Open, or first, position works a range from the open strings to the fifth fret. It contains the lowest notes playable on the guitar. Each finger has a fret position, with the open strings used instead of a first-finger stretch, and the fourth finger working both the fourth and fifth frets.

The Open Position

The Sixth String: E, F, and G

All of the notes found in open position can also be found in the fifth position—except for the notes on the sixth string. These will be the first notes that we learn in the open position: E below the third ledger line, F on the third ledger line, and G below the second ledger line.

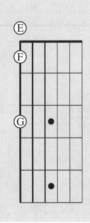

EXERCISE 1: Sixth String

The Fifth String: A, B, and C

We are already familiar with these notes from playing them at the fifth position, on the sixth string. Now we will learn to play them in open position on the fifth string: A on the open fifth string, B at the second fret, and C at the third fret.

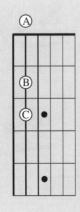

EXERCISE 2: Fifth String

EXERCISE 3: Fifth and Sixth Strings

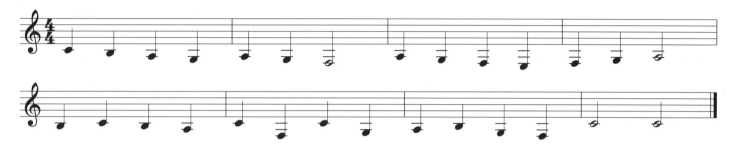

The Fourth String: D, E, and F

We already know these notes from the fifth position, on the fifth string. Now we will play them in open position on the fourth string: D on the open fourth string, E on the second fret, and F on the third fret.

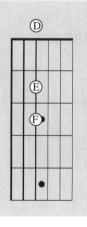

EXERCISE 4: Fourth String

EXERCISE 5: Fourth and Fifth Strings

Open Position Melodies

EXERCISE 1

EXERCISE 2

EXERCISE 3

EXERCISE 4

EXERCISE 5

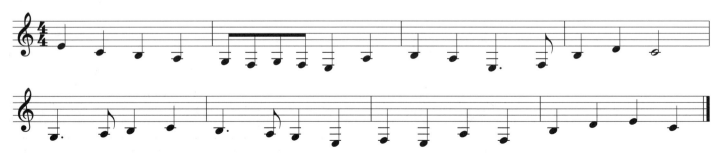

EXERCISE 6

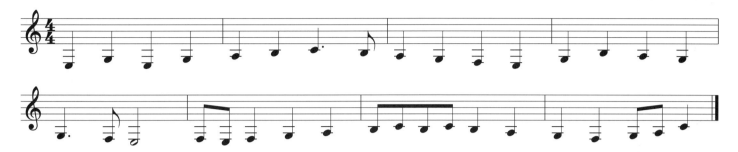

EXERCISE 7

EXERCISE 8

More Fifth Position Review

LONDONDERRY AIR

TRAD.

BOURREE

J.S. Bach

MELODY

Beethoven

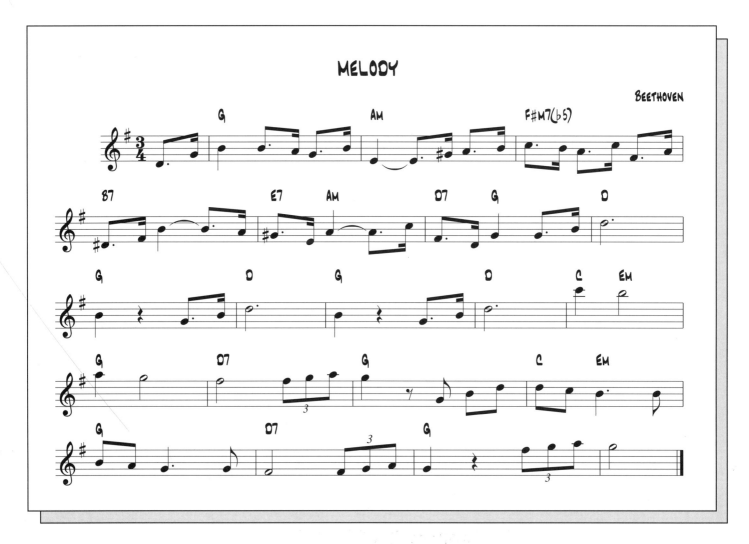

EXCERPT FROM A MINUET

Mozart

PRELUDE

Chopin

The *fermata* (⌢), sometimes called a bird's eye, tells you to hold a note and let time stop underneath it. You actually stop counting when you reach a fermata. The basic idea is to let the music breathe.

LULLABY

Brahms

SYMPHONIC THEME

Franck

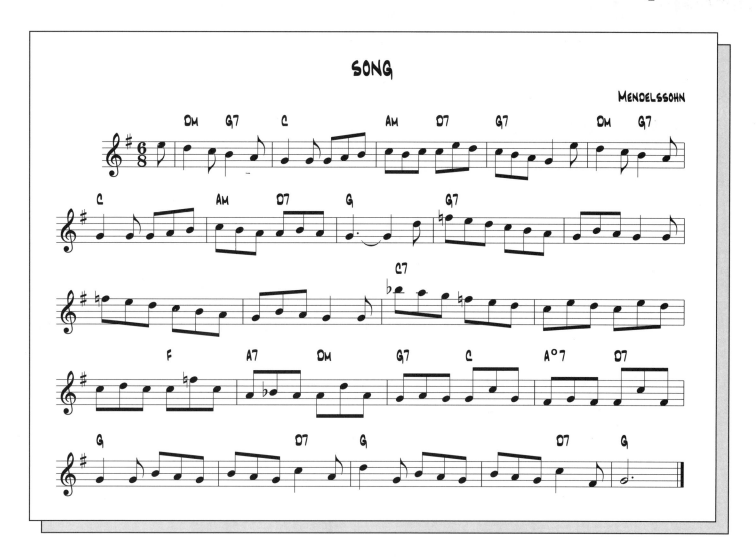

SONG

Mendelssohn

SYMPHONIC THEME

Schubert

Chapter Six

6

Rhythm Review—Picking Directions

Quarter notes will always be played with downstrokes. Synchronize your foot with the downstrokes of the pick.

Eighth notes will be played with a combination of downstrokes and upstrokes. Use alternate picking whenever possible.

Eighth-note triplets will be played with down- and upstrokes. Alternate picking will necessitate playing some upstrokes on strong beats and some downstrokes on weak beats, if there is more than one group of triplets.

Eighth-note triplet subdivisions will be picked using alternate picking. Count all three parts of the beat.

Sixteenth notes will always be played using alternate picking. In any type of sixteenth-note rhythmic figure, all four parts of the beat should be counted.

Rests do not change pick direction. Always see the rest as part of the rhythmic figure, and pick accordingly.

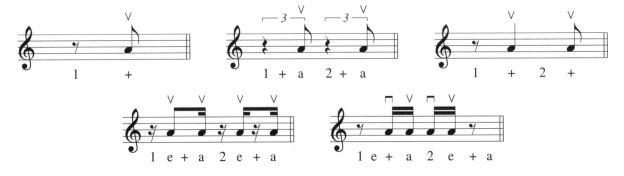

Mixed Rhythm Exercises

EXERCISE 1

EXERCISE 2

EXERCISE 3

EXERCISE 4

EXERCISE 5

EXERCISE 6

EXERCISE 7

EXERCISE 8

EXERCISE 9

EXERCISE 10

More Notes in Open Position

The Third String: G and A

We have already played these notes at the fifth position on the fourth string. Now we will learn them in open position, on the third string: G on the open third string and A at the second fret.

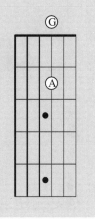

EXERCISE: Third and Fourth Strings

SYMPHONIC THEME

BRAHMS

THE DRUNKEN SAILOR

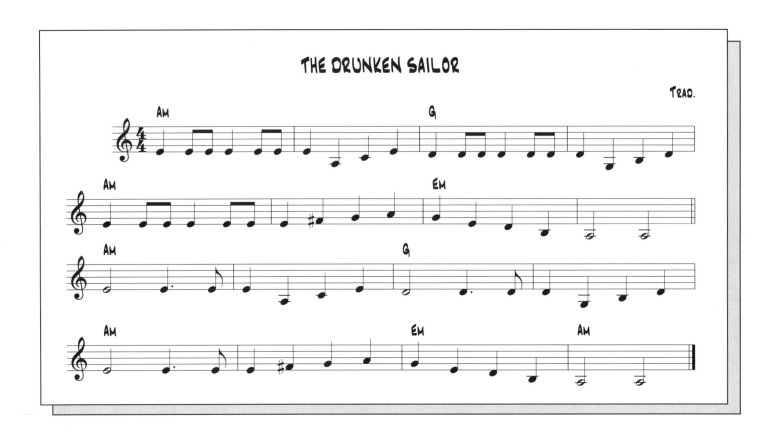

THE RAKES OF MALLOW

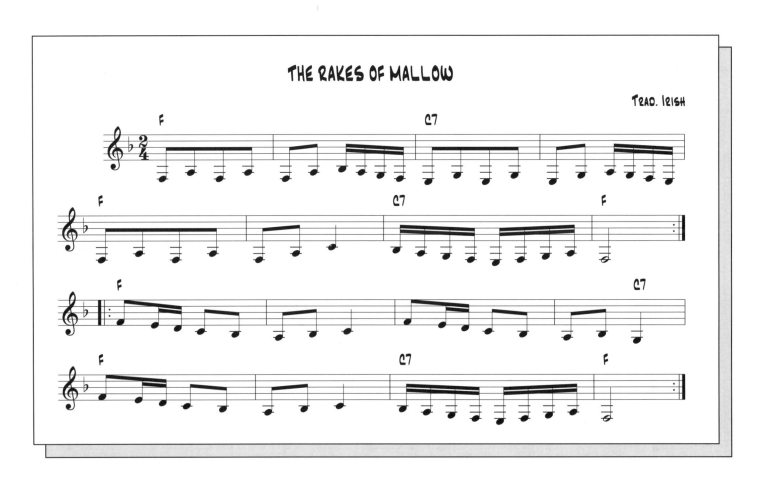

The Second String: B, C, and D

We are familiar with these notes at the fifth position, on the third string. Now we will play them in open position on the second string: B on the open second string, C at the first fret, and D at the third fret.

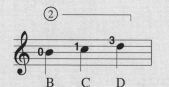

EXERCISE: Second- and Third-String Melody

The First String: E, F, and G

We have played these notes at the fifth position on the second string. Now we will play them in open position on the first string: E on the open first string, F at the first fret, and G at the third fret.

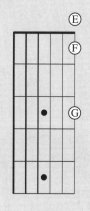

FUR ELISE

Beethoven

MINUET

J.S. Bach

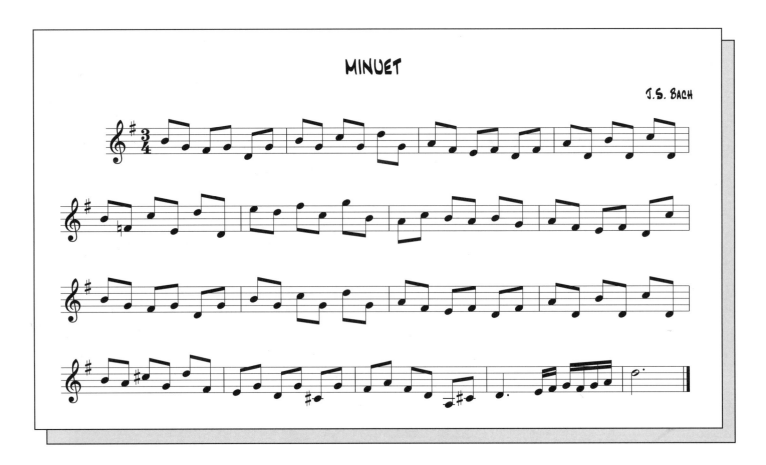

Expanding the Range of the Fifth Position

When the range of a melody briefly exceeds the range of the fifth position, for one or two notes, we can respond by temporarily extending our fingering range and then returning back to position. This happens often in the fifth position with the note D written above the staff. Technically, this note is not part of the fifth position, but it is OK to jump up for the note and then move back into position. Similarly, the low G, written below the staff, can be reached from the fifth position if we temporarily jump downward and then return back to position.

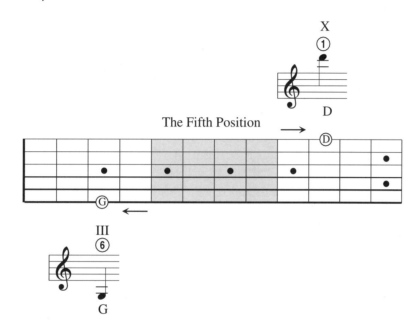

EXERCISE

VIOLIN EXCERPT

J.S. BACH

BOURREE
Guitar 1

J.S. BACH

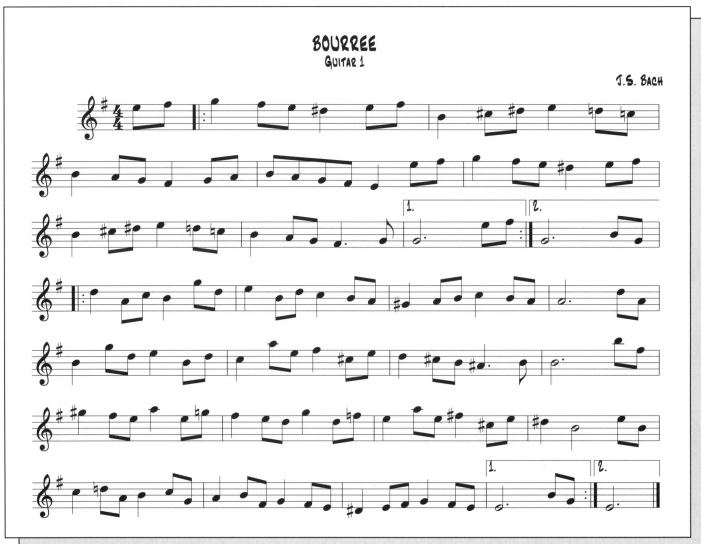

BOURREE
GUITAR 2

J.S. BACH

FANTASIE IMPROMPTU

Chopin

Chapter Seven

7

Introducing the Twelfth Position

We have already learned about ledger lines and used them from the low E below the staff to the high D above it. This chapter, we'll expand our ledger line reading to the fourth ledger line above the staff. To do this, we will begin to read in the *twelfth position.*

One of the easiest ways to learn the notes in the twelfth position is to pretend that you are still in open position. All the notes are one octave higher, but otherwise they are identical.

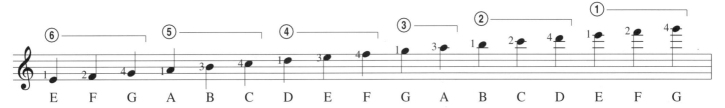

E F G A B C D E F G A B C D E F G

The hardest part of learning the twelfth position is losing your place inside the higher ledger lines. You will soon memorize these lines, but until then, here is a simple solution. You already know that the notes on the lines of the treble clef are E, G, B, D, and G and that the notes on the spaces are F, A, C, and E. Develop the technique of tracking your eye across the third ledger line—E on the first string, twelfth fret— then place an imaginary staff across that line to see the higher notes.

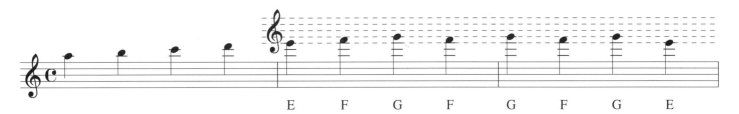

E F G F G F G E

EXERCISE 1: Fifth and Sixth Strings

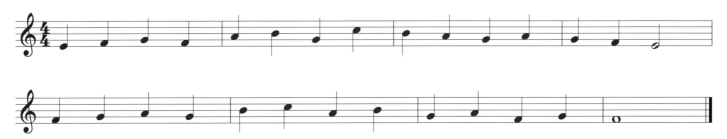

EXERCISE 2: Fifth and Sixth Strings

EXERCISE 3: Fourth and Fifth Strings

EXERCISE 4: Lower Strings

EXERCISE 5: Third and Fourth Strings

EXERCISE 6: Second and Third Strings

EXERCISE 7: First String

EXERCISE 8: Higher Strings

DUET

Mozart

Fifth and Open Position Review

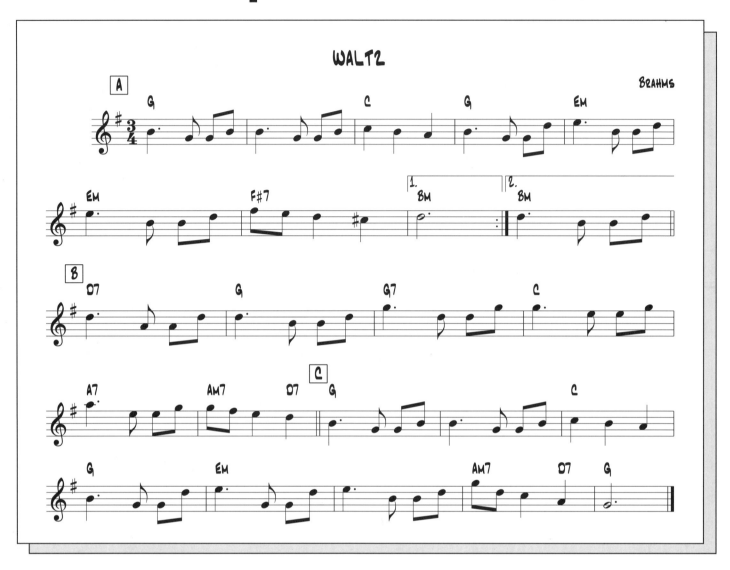

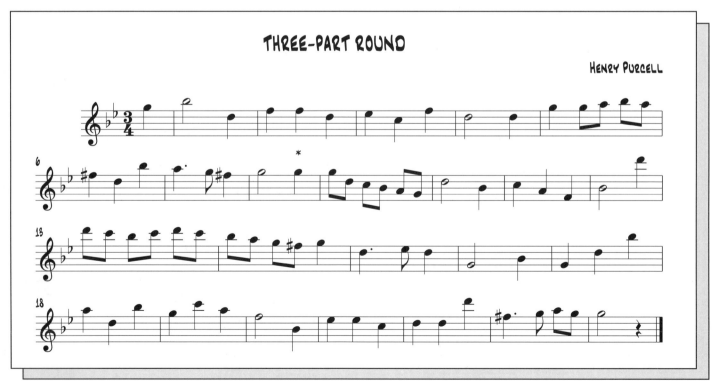

MINUETTO

Boccherini

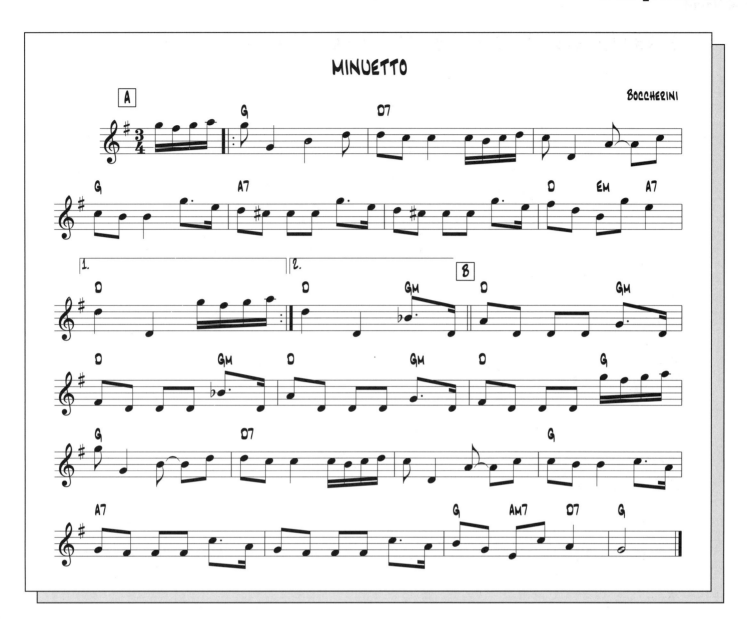

MY LODGING, IT'S COLD ON THE GROUND

Matthew Locke

BLACK IS THE COLOR

TRAD.

ORCHESTRAL EXCERPT

TCHAIKOVSKY

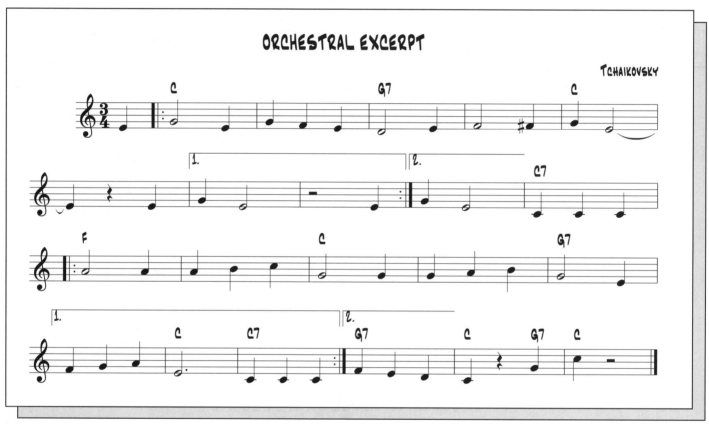

SYMPHONIC THEME

ANTON DVORAK

PIANO PRELUDE

Chopin

BEAUTIFUL DREAMER

Stephen Foster

GERMAN DANCE

Beethoven

DANCE

GRIEG

Sightreading vs. Prepared Reading

Remember the statement made in the preface to this book? *No one ever learned to sightread just by practicing sightreading.* You need to learn a lot of music from paper to develop reading skills. The next pages contain melodies originally written for the clavier, violin, or cello by the great composer Johann Sebastian Bach. These melodies contain large intervallic leaps, challenging key signatures, arpeggios, scales, and chromatic tones which make them difficult to sightread, but with the skills you have learned up to this point, they should not be too hard to learn; they can be played in the fifth position.

Begin slow. As you continue to work up these melodies, you will begin to hear the "implied harmony" in the music; when you reach this point, you are playing at an appropriate tempo. This will take a lot of practice and repetition. Be patient with yourself, and realize that this kind of reinforcement is crucial to developing reading skills.

J.S. BACH

J.S. BACH

J.S. BACH

These next few melodies are much simpler; try sightreading them in the fifth position. First, take a minute to look them over. Find the highest and lowest pitch. Look at the key signature. Watch for any tricky rhythms or wide interval leaps. Then start playing.

EXERCISE 1

EXERCISE 2

EXERCISE 3

Chapter Eight

8

 Quarter-Note Triplets

Just as an eighth-note triplet equals one quarter note, a *quarter-note triplet* equals one half note—or two quarter notes. This is also known as "three against two." Quarter-note triplets are a bit difficult to count at first, but with practice they will become easier. The first part of learning how to count quarter-note triplets is understanding how three can divide evenly into two. What is the common denominator between three and two? The answer is six.

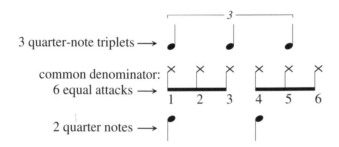

If the quarter-note pulse (at the bottom of the figure above) is subdivided in three, and felt as eighth-note triplets, six attacks are created. Each note of the quarter-note triplet (at the top of the figure above) will then equal two of these attacks.

The next problem is counting and playing the quarter-note triplets while feeling the quarter-note pulse. A great way to do this is to break the rhythm down into different actions and coordinations. Break down these coordinated actions first out of time, then gradually build the coordination up in time until you can count quarter-note triplets while clapping and keeping the quarter-note pulse with your foot. Be patient.

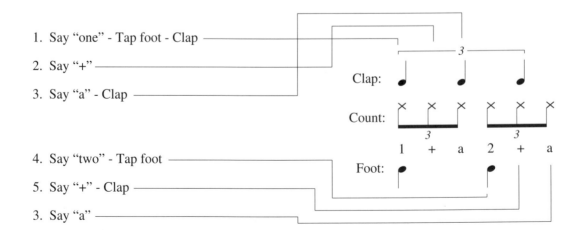

1. Say "one" - Tap foot - Clap
2. Say "+"
3. Say "a" - Clap
4. Say "two" - Tap foot
5. Say "+" - Clap
3. Say "a"

Mixed Rhythm Exercises

EXERCISE 1

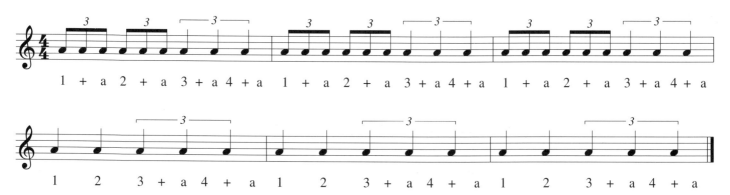

EXERCISE 2

EXERCISE 3

EXERCISE 4

EXERCISE 5

EXERCISE 6

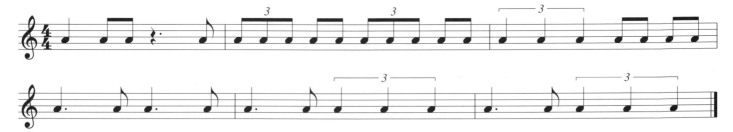

EXERCISE 7

EXERCISE 8

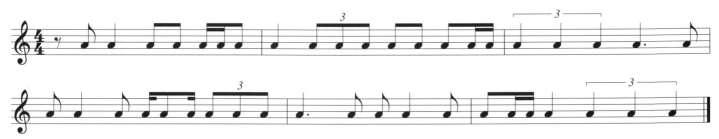

Scales in Rhythm—C Major

Set your metronome at a constant tempo. Use alternate picking. Try these rhythms with different scale patterns.

Introduction to Reading 8va in Fifth Position

The symbol *8va* is an abbreviation of "ottava," or octave. It is used in written music to indicate that a part should be read *one octave higher* than it is actually notated. This symbol is written above the staff that it affects and generally remains in effect until the word *loco,* an Italian term that means "in place."

There are a number of reasons why it is important to learn to read an octave higher than written. For one thing, the guitar actually sounds *one octave lower* than written. The note C, for instance, written on the third space of the staff, when played on guitar actually sounds as the the note "middle C" on the first ledger line below the staff.

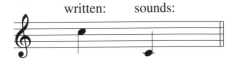

Some practical reasons for reading one octave higher, or *8va,* include:

- To save a guitarist from reading lots and lots of ledger lines.
- To help a guitarist bring out the melody in relation to other instruments when playing in an ensemble.
- To help a guitarist blend better with other instruments in an ensemble.

As we've already learned, the fifth position is the best place on the guitar to read a melody—the intonation is better there, and the tone also is fuller. So let's begin reading *8va* in the fifth position:

ENGLISH FOLK SONG

SYMPHONIC THEME

Dvorak

CAPRICCIO

Tchaikovsky

REVERIE

Review of the Open, Fifth, and Twelfth Positions

The open or first position contains all the notes played on the first four frets of the guitar, including the open strings and a fourth-finger stretch to the fifth fret. Below is a chart that shows all the natural notes (strings and fingerings) in the open or first position.

EXERCISE 1: B♭ Major, Open Position

EXERCISE 2: A♭ Major, Open Position

EXERCISE 3: D♭ Major, Open Position

The fifth position contains all the notes from the fifth to the eighth fret, including a first-finger stretch to the fourth fret and a fourth-finger stretch to the ninth fret. Below is a chart showing all the natural notes (strings and fingerings) in the fifth position.

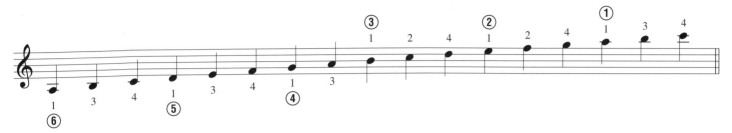

EXERCISE 4

EXERCISE 5

EXERCISE 5 (cont'd)

EXERCISE 6

The twelfth position contains all the notes from the twelfth fret to the fifteenth fret of the guitar, including a first-finger stretch to the eleventh fret and a fourth-finger stretch to the sixteenth fret. Below is a chart showing all the natural notes (strings and fingerings) in the twelfth position.

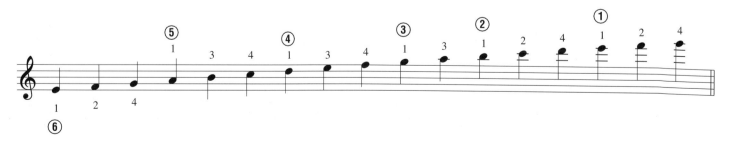

EXERCISE 7

EXERCISE 8

EXERCISE 9

Chapter Nine

9

Cut Time

Cut time is a common name given to the 2/2 time signature. In 2/2 or cut time, there are two beats in a measure, and the half note gets one beat. This requires the foot to tap only two beats in each measure.

When the half note gets the beat, all rhythmic values tend to feel different from the "4/4" values that we are used to: the whole note feels like a half note, the half note feels like a quarter note, the quarter note feels like an eighth note, etc.

Cut time is used often in popular commercial music. It helps to slow down the basic pulse of a song for the performers while keeping the energy or tempo of the song fast or up. There are many famous examples of cut time. Here are just a few:

As you can see in these examples, measure for measure, cut time looks exactly like 4/4 time. Play the above examples again in 4/4, keeping the tempo the same. Notice any stress from tapping your foot so quickly? Now play the examples again with a cut time feel. Cut time greatly reduces the amount of stress involved in playing at faster tempos. Picking directions for cut time should feel like those in common time; play downstrokes on all half notes or strong beats, and play upstrokes on all weak beats.

Mixed Rhythm Exercises

EXERCISE 1

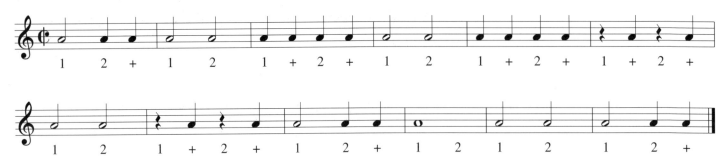

EXERCISE 2

EXERCISE 3

Introducing the Second Position

The *second position* is located halfway between open position and fifth position. It can be used as a bridge between these two popular positions and is very easy to learn because it contains all the notes that we have learned up to this point. Second position does not officially contain any open strings; however, they are often used for effect.

The Second Position

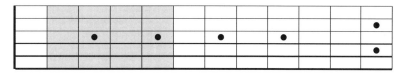

Second position is often thought of as a sharp-key reading area; the keys of D major, C major, A major, G major, and E major all lie fairly well within this position. Not coincidentally, the open strings are diatonic to most of these scale patterns; this is why combining open strings with the second position is usually effective. *Timbre* is a word that defines quality of tone. Notes or phrases can have a dark timbre, or a bright timbre. Using open strings in the second position can give a note or phrase a ringing, sustaining, or harp-like timbre.

D, E, F♯, G, and A

We will begin learning the second position with the notes D, E, F♯, G, and A. The notes D and E are played on the second string, while F♯, G, and A are located on the first string.

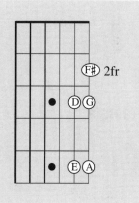

EXERCISE 1

EXERCISE 2

EXERCISE 2 (cont'd)

A, B, C#, and G#

We will continue learning the second position by adding the notes A, B, C#, and G#. A and B are played on the third string; C#, on the second string; and G# on the first.

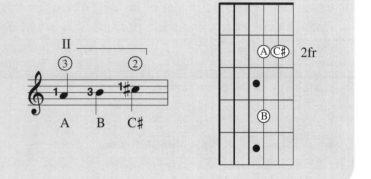

EXERCISE 3

EXERCISE 4

Much like the note B in the fifth position, the note F on the fifth line of the staff does not fall into the second position without either a slight finger stretch or a position shift. Here are a few possiblilities for dealing with this note. Watch the fingerings.

EXERCISE 5: Position Shift

EXERCISE 6: First-Finger Stretch

Choosing a Playing Position

How does one decide when to use a particular position on the guitar? Unfortunately, there are no cut and dry answers. And when sightreading, these decisions must be made quickly. Here are a few rough guidelines:

- If you are playing a melody with a band backing you up, consider playing in the middle of the neck and possibly an octave higher than written.
- If you are playing an accompanimental part, examine the part for implied harmony. Consider playing the notes in an area of the guitar neck where you can let the notes ring, possibly using open strings to enhance this timbre.
- If there are phrase markings asking for hammer-ons, pull-offs, slides, trills, or string bends, try to find a position on the guitar that will make these phrase markings happen.
- If you are in a high-pressure sightreading situation, visualize the highest and lowest notes of the piece, and let that determine your reading position. (This may not be the most musical way to read, but no one will ever fault you for doing it.)

Ultimately, the way we want to express a musical phrase should determine our fingering and position decisions, and experience is the best guide. Remember that there are many guitarists who can sightread but very few who can sightread musically.

Play this melody in the second position. Don't be afraid to use open strings for a ringing timbre.

POMP AND CIRCUMSTANCE

Sir Edward Elgar

Play in the open position...

Shift to the 2nd position...

Shift to the 5th position...

Play this melody in the open position, in the fifth position, and in the fifth position *8va*.

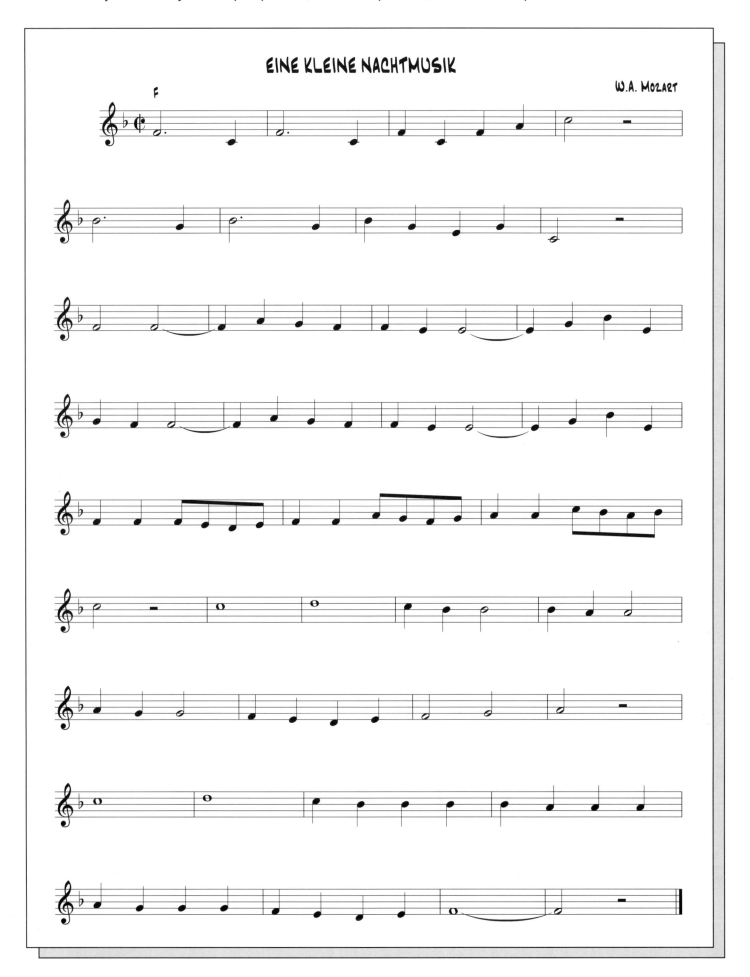

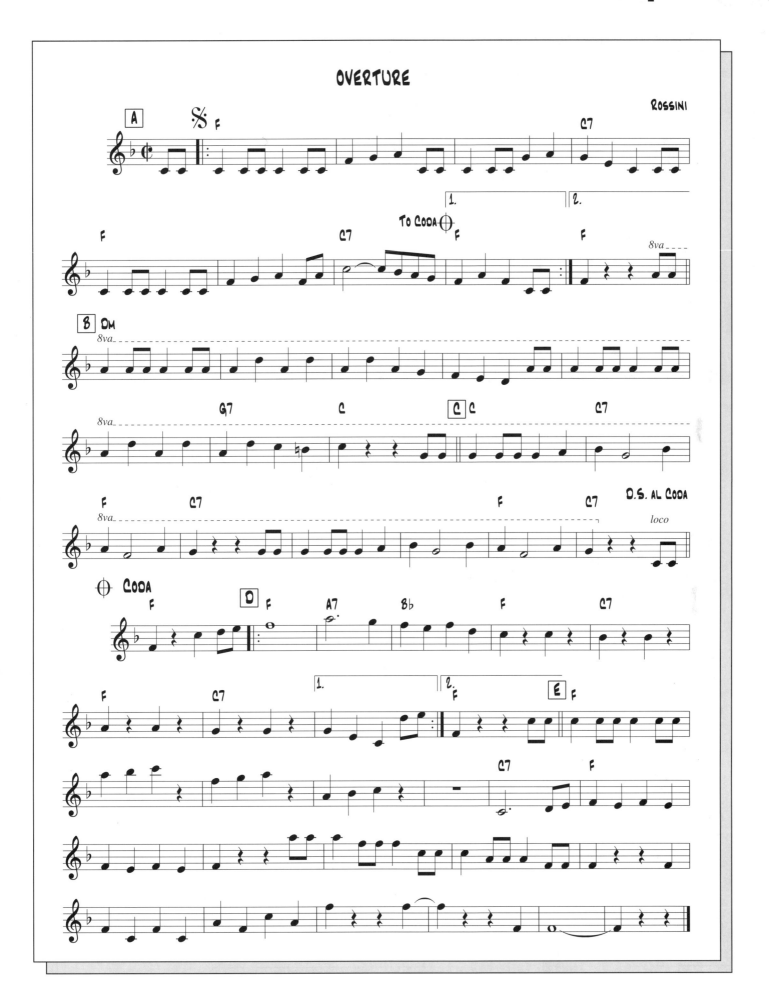

OVERTURE

EXCERPT IN C

J.S. BACH

EXCERPT IN C MINOR

J.S. BACH

EXCERPT IN D MINOR

J.S. Bach

Chapter Ten

 Half-Note Triplets

Half-note triplets are really quite similar to quarter-note triplets. More often than not in fact, you will encounter half-note triplets in cut time, in which case they are counted and felt exactly as quarter-note triplets are counted in common time.

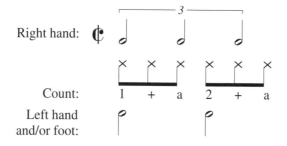

Right hand:

Count: 1   +   a   2   +   a

Left hand and/or foot:

In common time, half-note triplets take on a "three against four" character.

 Sixteenth-Note Triplets

Two sixteenth notes normally occupy the same amount of time as one eighth note. Any duple time value, however, can be divided into three equal parts instead. An eighth note divided into three equal parts forms a *sixteenth-note triplet.*

1   +   2   e   +   a   3   t   t   +   4   +   t   t

Mixed Rhythm Exercises

EXERCISE 1

EXERCISE 2

EXERCISE 3

EXERCISE 4

EXERCISE 5

EXERCISE 6

EXERCISE 7

EXERCISE 8

EXERCISE 9

EXERCISE 10

EXERCISE 11

EXERCISE 12

More Notes in Second Position

We will continue learning the second position by focusing on its lower octave. We have played all of these notes previously in either the fifth or open position, but the following studies will help you learn and memorize the notes in their second position fingerings. Work several different exercises each day.

D, E, F♯, and G

The notes E, F♯, and G can be found on the fourth string, while the note D is located on the fifth.

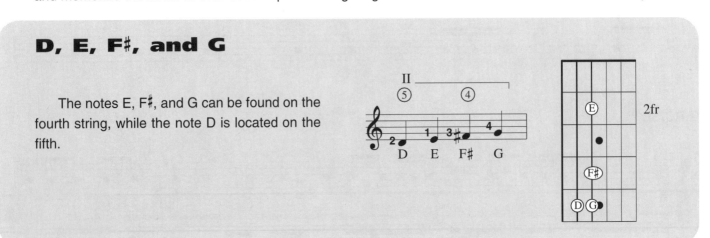

EXERCISE 1

EXERCISE 2

EXERCISE 3

EXERCISE 4

EXERCISE 5

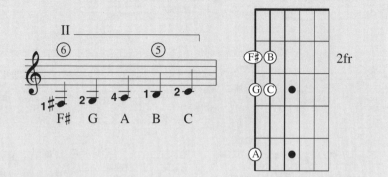

Lower Ledger Lines: F♯, G, A, B, and C

We will finish the second position with the notes found on lower ledger lines: F♯, G, A, B, and C. The notes F♯, G, and A are located on the sixth string; the notes B and C are located on the fifth string.

EXERCISE 6

EXERCISE 7

Position Review

The following melodies can be read many different ways. Try them in the second, fifth, and open positions as well as, wherever possible, in fifth position 8va. Look for places to make musical shifts in reading positions: If the melody is ascending in a pattern, then look for ways to shift up to the next position; if it is descending, look for possible ways to shift downward. Consider using open strings to change the timbre of the melody. With each melody, work the tempos up so that you can hear the phrasing.

DANCE

Tchaikovsky

AYLESFORD GAVOTTE

G.F. Handel

(CONT'D)

AYLESFORD GAVOTTE (CONT'D)

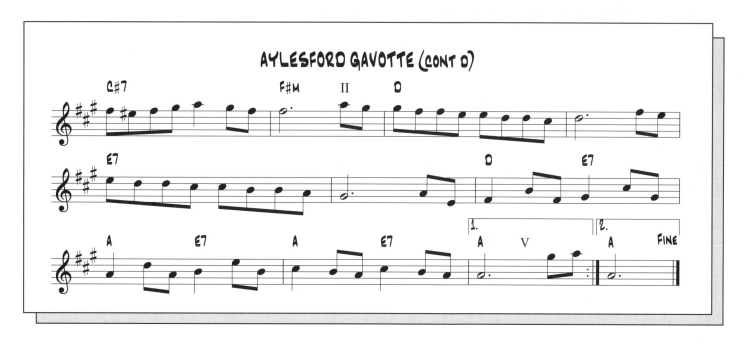

BOURREE

G.F. HANDEL

Chapter Eleven

 Thirty-Second Notes

Until now, the smallest division of the quarter note that we have worked on has been the sixteenth note. We will now begin learning how to count and feel the *thirty-second note*. Just as two sixteenth notes equal one eighth note, two thirty-second notes equal one sixteenth note. To count thirty-second notes, use the syllable "ta."

1   + t t t

Many times when we see thirty-second notes, we assume that they must be played very fast. While this is true in some instances, most music that involves thirty-second notes is intended to be played at a slower tempo. Clap the following rhythm at a comfortable tempo, counting out loud and tapping the eighth note as the pulse.

Mixed Rhythm Exercises

EXERCISE 1

EXERCISE 2

EXERCISE 3

EXERCISE 4

EXERCISE 5

EXERCISE 6

EXERCISE 7

EXERCISE 8

EXERCISE 9

EXERCISE 10

EXERCISE 11

EXERCISE 12

EXERCISE 13

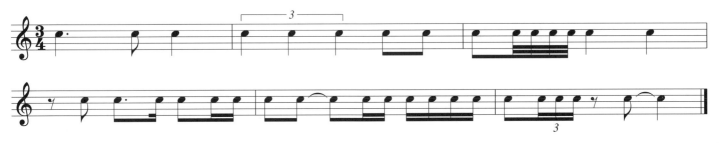

Scales in Rhythm—B♭ Major

Practice each line until you can play it evenly, ascending and descending. Then practice the entire set without breaking your tempo. Alternate pick each line. This exercise will help you learn to shift from eighths to triplets to sixteenths to thirty-seconds without shifting tempo.

Working these rhythms in scale patterns or repeated-note studies will also help to internalize the feel of sixteenth-note triplets and thirty-second notes.

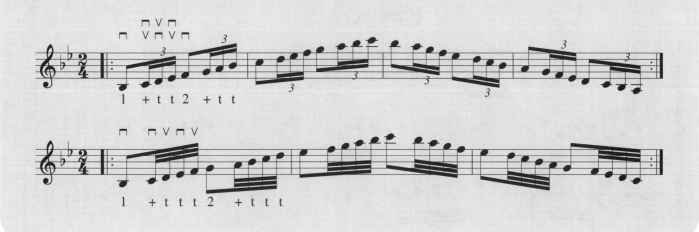

Phrasing

Previously, we learned that a tie is a curved line that connects two notes of the same pitch. Sometimes, we see a curved line connecting two or more notes of different pitches. This is a type of phrase marking called a *slur*. The Italian term for a slur is *legato,* which means smooth or connected.

When two notes are connected with a slur, a guitarist can use hammer-ons, pull-offs, slides, or string bends to connect the notes. Sometimes the technique is specified, and sometimes it is not. If the second pitch is higher than the first, use a hammer-on, slide, or string bend. If the second pitch is lower than the first, use a pull-off, slide, or reverse bend. If more than two notes are connected with a slur, try to connect the entire phrase as smoothly as possible.

When trying to decide which position to use for a given melody, consider the phrasing. If a piece employs specific phrase markings like slurs, find a position that will make those markings happen. The following examples all contain phrase markings; the fingering positions are marked and explained.

Play the Toreador's Song in the second position. Use hammer-ons and pull-offs in the last system. These phrasing marks lay well in the second position; in the fifth position, they would be practically impossible without awkward finger stretches.

Read "Riffin' in C" in the fifth position. Work out the notes and rhythms. You can play this example with a sixteenth-note shuffle or straight. After you have worked it out, turn the page and read it again with the suggested phrasing. Compare the two.

Pay close attention to the fingerings and phrasings marked. Practice them until they feel comfortable.

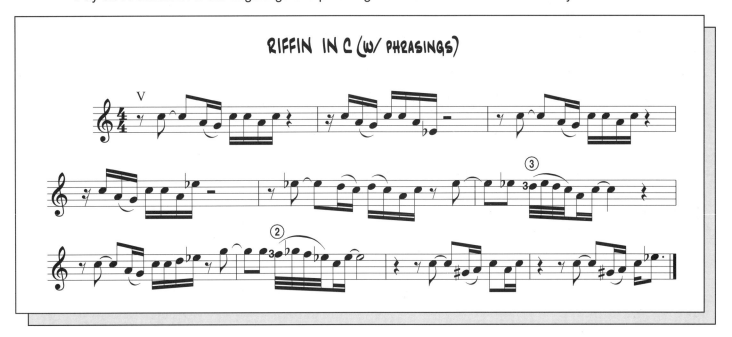

RIFFIN IN C (W/ PHRASINGS)

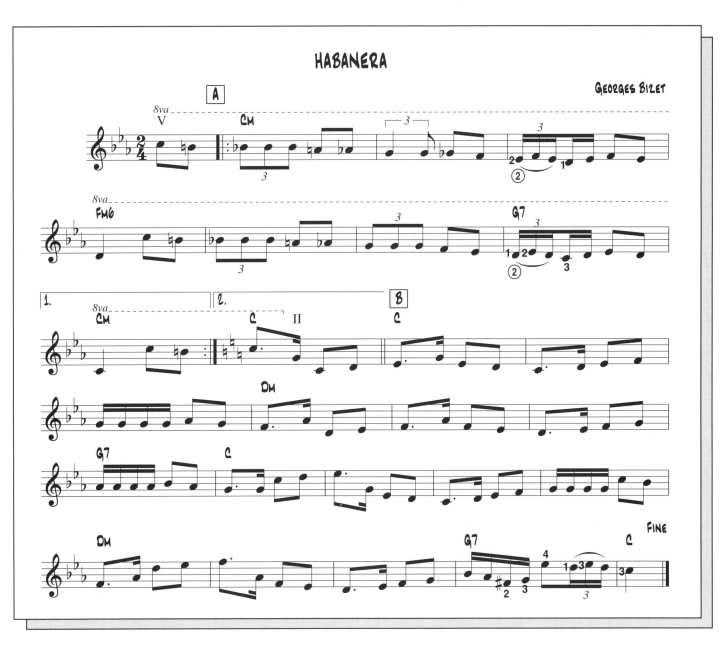

HABANERA

GEORGES BIZET

SYMPHONY THEME

W.A. Mozart

DUET
Guitar 1
Watch out for all position shifts and follow the left hand fingerings

Guitar 2
Play this part in the 2nd position

This piece uses many of the techniques that we have talked about in the past few chapters. It incorporates the use of the second position as well as the fifth position. It also uses phrase markings, thirty-second notes, and the timbre of open strings within the second position. The tempo of this piece was originally intended to be very slow, but as guitar players, we will need to play it faster than violinists do—to compensate for our lack of sustain.

This piece can be played as a solo exercise, but it is intended as three-part canon. When guitar 1 reaches measure 3, guitar 2 should start in from the beginning, and when guitar 2 reaches measure 3, guitar 3 should step in from the beginning. Check the last two staves to see where everyone ends.

CANON IN D

Johann Pachelbel

Shifting Positions—The Pipeline

Frequently, it is desirable to shift out of home position for a passage. While this is an almost constant occurrence in chordal reading, there are several situations you will encounter in single-note melodic reading as well.

Sometimes, a part encompasses a greater range than can be found in any one position.

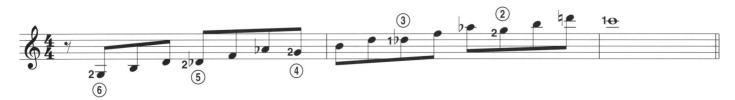

Here is another example of position shifting through a wide range, using just the first and fourth finger of the left hand.

Another common situation calling for position shifting involves larger melodic intervals. These intervallic lines sometimes lay much more comfortably when the intervals are played along a string pair, even though the pitches could be made to fit within a single position.

Other times, a melody calls for a specific timbre and the player must shift position to play a give pitch on a specific string.

Single-string reading can be a great antidote to position reading. I find it particularly useful in the upper regions of the fingerboard, when working between the fifth and twelfth positions—an area I like to call "The Pipeline."

Play only on the first string:

EXERCISE 1

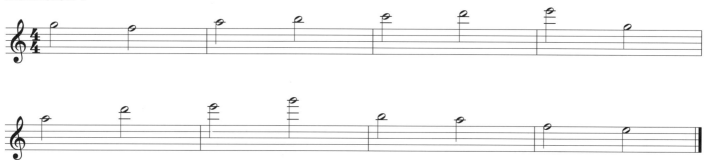

Play only on the second string:

EXERCISE 2

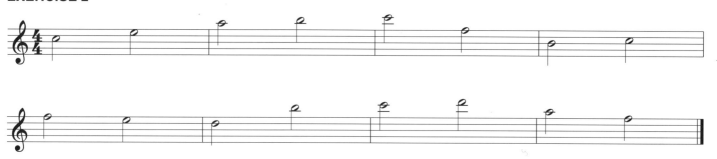

Play only on the third string:

EXERCISE 3

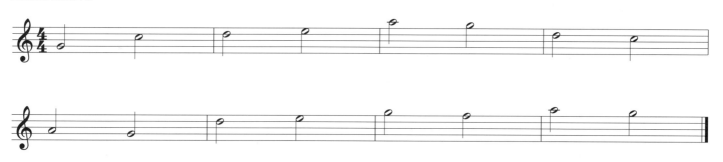

Play only on the fourth string:

EXERCISE 4

Read up and down the first and second strings:

EXERCISE 5

Read up and down the second and third strings:

EXERCISE 6

Read up and down the third and fourth strings:

EXERCISE 7

Read up and down the fourth and fifth strings:

EXERCISE 8

It's been my experience that many guitarists have a hard time trusting themselves to read up and down the fingerboard. However, with practice, this technique can be achieved. The previous exercises are just the beginning. Go back through this book, and read as many exercises as you can over again. Look at the range of the melody. The high and low notes will tell you which string or string sets will work. Remember that reading up and down the fingerboard is one of the most musically expressive ways to read. I've said it before, and I'll say it again: "There are many guitarists out there who can read music, but only a few who can read musically!"

Chapter Twelve

3/4 Time in "One"

Meter is a regularly occurring set of strong and weak beats that occur in a piece of music. 3/4 is a simple triple meter, which is generally felt as "STRONG-weak-weak." Though the normal way to count 3/4 time is to tap the foot three times per measure and to assign each tap a quarter value, 3/4 can also be felt in one. When 3/4 is felt in one, the entire measure occurs within a single beat—the dotted half note.

Mixed Rhythm Exercises

Practice the following exercises, tapping the foot in "one" while counting in "three."

EXERCISE 1

EXERCISE 2

EXERCISE 3

EXERCISE 4

EXERCISE 5

EXERCISE 6

EXERCISE 7

EXERCISE 8

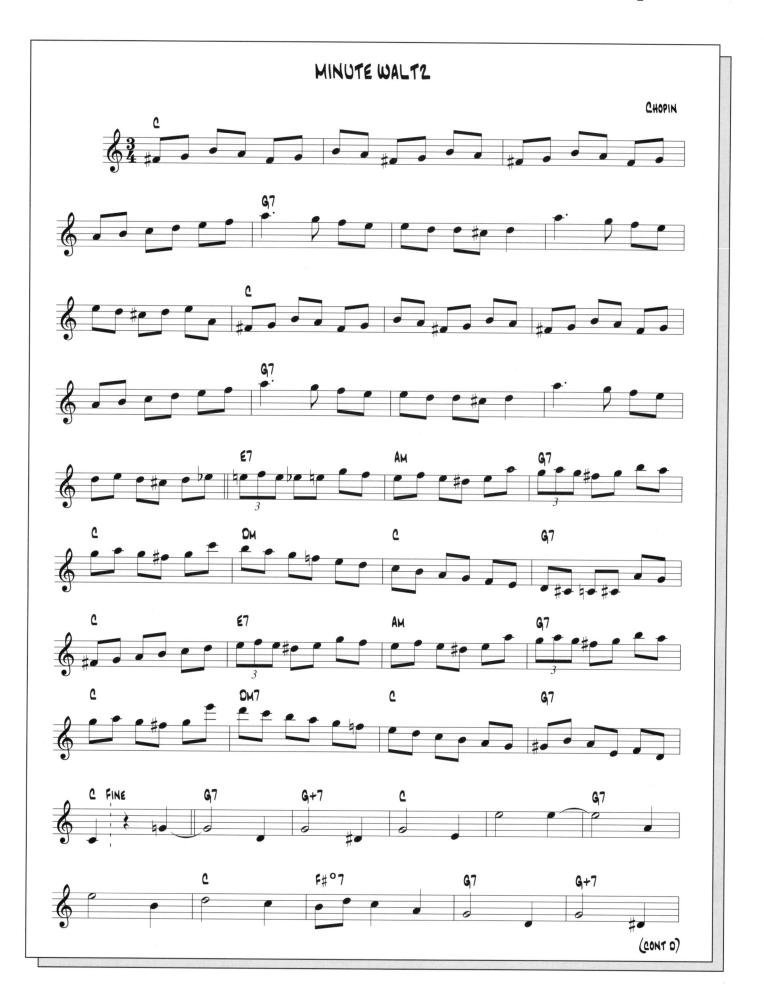

Reading an Implied Harmony

One way to read more musically on the guitar is to have an awareness of harmony. Many times, a melody will outline the chord changes going on around it. The reader needs to be able to make a quick analysis of these changes and then bring out this harmony while still playing the melody. Your left hand will be moving in chord shapes while your right hand will be picking out single notes.

Check out the figure below. Triads can be analyzed in each measure and then brought out in the line. Your position-shifting skills must be very strong to accomplish this.

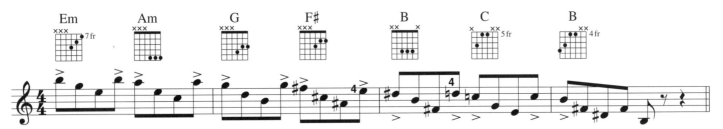

Notice that the accents in the above example point the way to the melody. We should make sure that these notes are brought out but not over-accented.

One of the best ways to develop this ability is to read the music of J.S. Bach. His single-line melodies always show an implied harmony. Check out this excerpt below, and then read the Gavotte duet on the following pages.

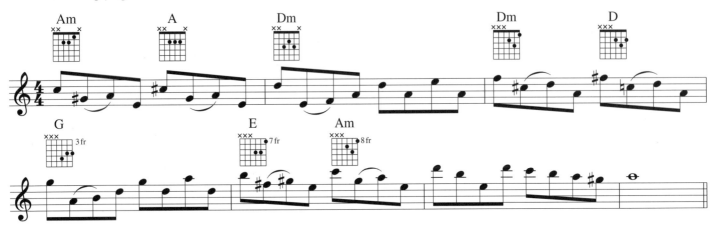

GAVOTTE
GUITAR 1

J.S. BACH

GAVOTTE
Guitar 2

J.S. Bach

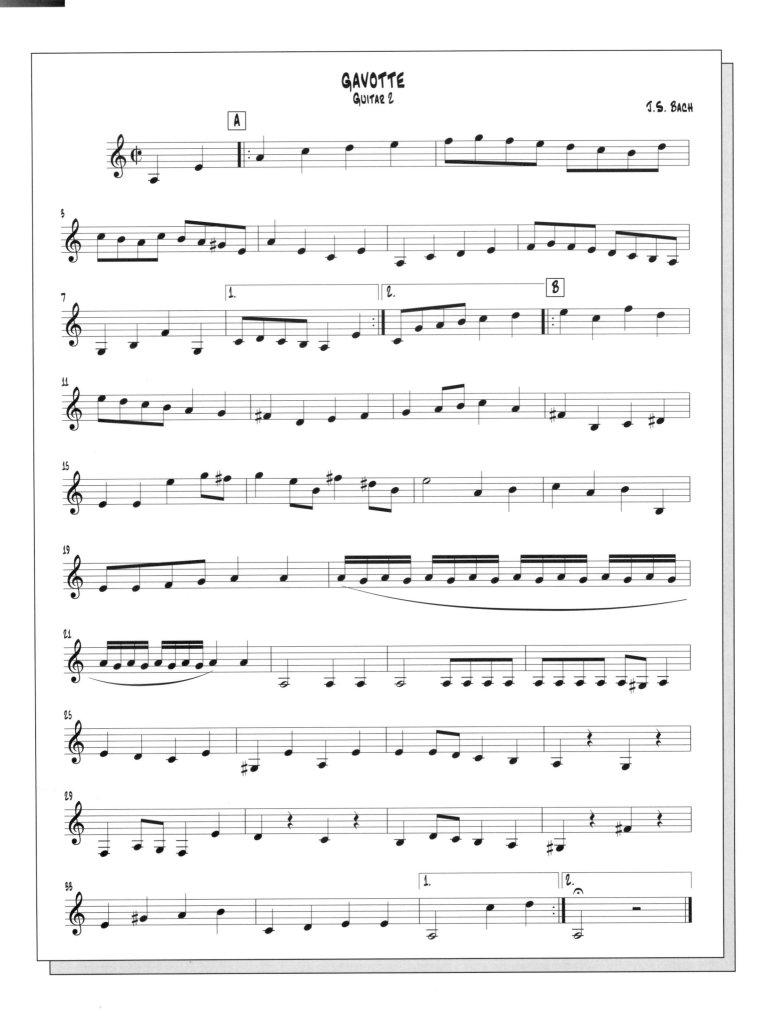

The Third Position

The third position is important for two reasons. First, if a melody is awkward to play in the fifth position, odds are that it will lie better in the third position. Second, the third position is an excellent place to read a flat-key melody on the guitar. The third position and its upper-neck counterpart, the eighth position, will always play second fiddle to the fifth position, but we still need to feel comfortable in these areas simply to be able to read potentially awkward melodies with more phrasing and musicality.

The Third Position

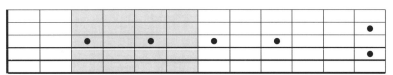

EXERCISE 1

EXERCISE 2

EXERCISE 3

EXERCISE 4

EXERCISE 5

EXERCISE 6

Chapter Thirteen

Changing Meters and Odd Meter

There are two important elements in learning how to shift between different meters. First, one needs to know what the rhythmic shift will sound like, and second, one needs to find the common denominator of the rhythm. We will focus here on rhythms that shift between 3/4 and 6/8 time. The common denominator will be the eighth note. The foot will tap three times in 3/4 and twice in 6/8, but you will count the eighth-note constantly throughout both meters.

Mixed Rhythm Exercises

EXERCISE 1

EXERCISE 2

EXERCISE 3

Practice the rhythms of these first, then add the pitches.

EXERCISE 4

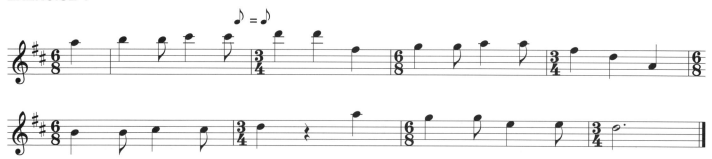

EXERCISE 5

EXERCISE 6

Two-Part Rhythmic Coordination

Rhythm-reading skills don't stop with the thirty-second-note subdivision; we need to continue drilling and becoming more comfortable with rhythm. One of the most important aspects of having a good sense of time is developing two-part coordination. Practice the following exercises, singing the top line while clapping the bottom line. Tap your foot with the quarter-note pulse.

Two-Part Rhythmic Coordination (cont'd)

More on Phrasing and Position Shifting

Look at the following excerpt. The tempo is fast and the melody seems to develop the same motive or idea. If we played this excerpt in one position, we would have to phrase the motive differently each time we played it. In order to play the motive consistently, we need to be able to shift the idea around comfortably to different areas of the fingerboard. This would not only enable us to keep the timbre consistent from one phrase to the next, but also make the passage easier to play.

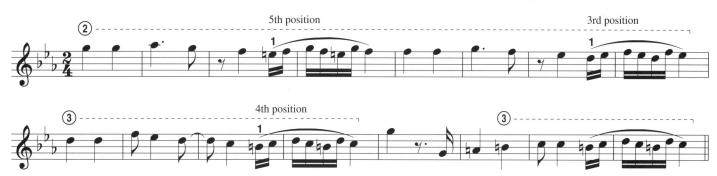

HUNGARIAN DANCE NO. 5

Brahms

The Seventh Position

To some extent, we have already read from the seventh position—in the position shifting exercises of previous chapters. Now, however, we will focus on it more fully.

The lower registers of the seventh position (strings 5 and 6) have a very dark timbre compared to the same notes in the fifth position. These lower notes in the seventh position and higher (eighth, ninth, and tenth positions) also tend to have intonation problems. The reader needs to take these elements into consideration before reading a melody in the upper positions. Usually, it will be more practical to shift up into the seventh position to reach higher notes, then shift back down. However, this does not mean that we are not going to learn these notes!

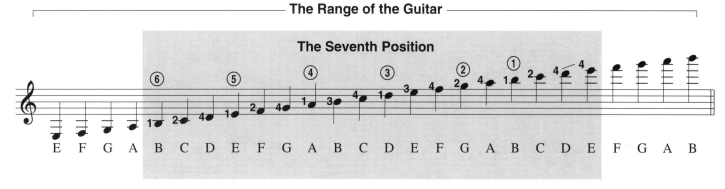

EXERCISE 1

EXERCISE 2

EXERCISE 3

The best way to learn a position is to learn to play something in its area of the fingerboard. Learn the next few melodies in the seventh position. Remember that the seventh position includes a first-finger stretch back to the sixth fret.

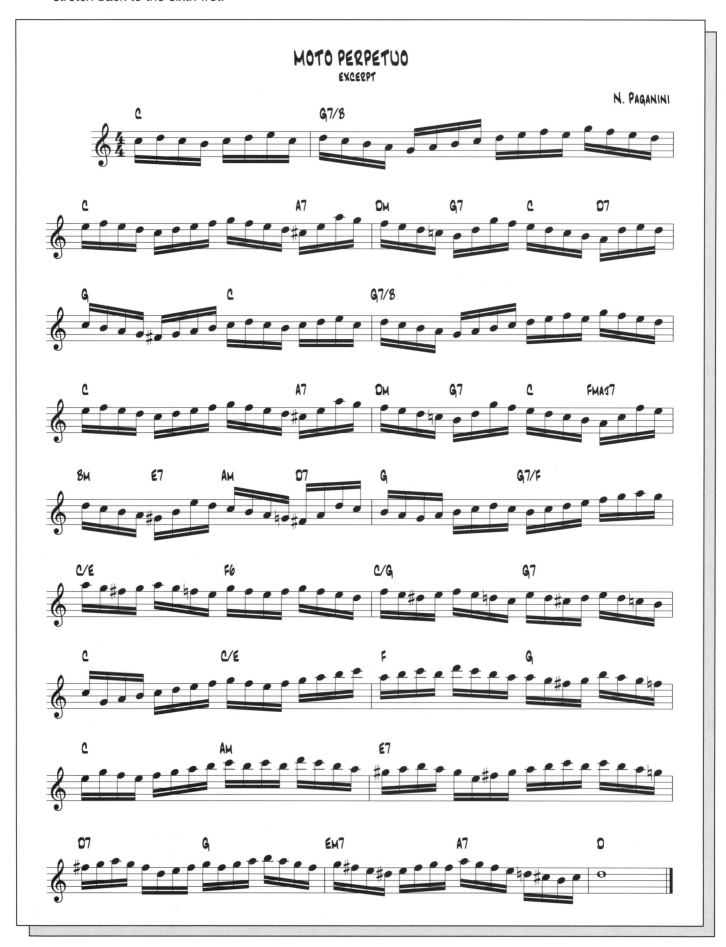

RONDO ALLA TURCA

MOZART

(CONT'D)

RONDO ALLA TURCA (CONT D)

DANCE OF THE REED FLUTES

Divisi means that two players will divide the parts up. One will take the notes stems up, and the other will take the notes stems down.

Try reading this tune in the seventh position, except for measures 23–25, which can be played down the first and second strings from the twelfth fret to the open position, and measures 26–29, which use the open third string between the open and twelfth positions. Why do it this way? Timbre!

Sightreading Review

Sightread the following exercises in fifth position.

EXERCISE 1

EXERCISE 2

EXERCISE 3

EXERCISE 4

Sightread these exercises in open position.

EXERCISE 5

EXERCISE 6

EXERCISE 7

EXERCISE 8

Sightread these in second position.

EXERCISE 9

EXERCISE 10

EXERCISE 11

EXERCISE 12

Sightread these in fifth position, one octave higher than written.

EXERCISE 13

EXERCISE 14

EXERCISE 15

EXERCISE 16